THE PELICAN SHAKESPEARE
GENERAL EDITORS

STEPHEN ORGEL
A. R. BRAUNMULLER

The Narrative Poems

Lucretia
An engraving after Raphael by
Marcantonio Raimondi, c. 1511–12

William Shakespeare

———

The Narrative Poems

EDITED BY JONATHAN CREWE

PENGUIN BOOKS

PENGUIN BOOKS
An imprint of Penguin Random House LLC
penguinrandomhouse.com

The Narrative Poems edited by Richard Wilbur published in
Penguin Books (USA) 1966
Revised edition edited by Richard Wilbur and
Alfred Harbage published 1974
Edition edited by Jonathan Crewe published 1999
This edition published 2020

Frontispiece: Gift of Mrs. T. Jefferson Coolidge.
Courtesy, Museum of Fine Arts, Boston

ISBN 978-0-14-071481-4

Printed in the United States of America

Set in Adobe Garamond
Designed by Virginia Norey

Contents

Publisher's Note   vii

The Theatrical World   ix

The Texts of Shakespeare   xxv

Introduction   xxix

Note on the Text   liii

The Narrative Poems

Venus and Adonis   2

Lucrece   49

The Phoenix and the Turtle   121

The Passionate Pilgrim   125

A Lover's Complaint   139

Publisher's Note

THE PELICAN SHAKESPEARE has served generations of readers as an authoritative series of texts and scholarship since the first volume appeared under the general editorship of Alfred Harbage over half a century ago. In the past decades, new editions followed to reflect the profound changes textual and critical studies of Shakespeare have undergone. The texts of the plays and poems were thoroughly revised in accordance with leading scholarship, and in some cases were entirely reedited. New introductions and notes were provided in all the volumes. The Pelican Shakespeare was designed as a successor to the original series; the previous editions had been taken into account, and the advice of the previous editors was solicited where it was feasible to do so. The current editions include updated bibliographic references to recent scholarship.

Certain textual features of the new Pelican Shakespeare should be particularly noted. All lines are numbered that contain a word, phrase, or allusion explained in the glossarial notes. In addition, for convenience, every tenth line is also numbered, in italics when no annotation is indicated. The intrusive and often inaccurate place headings inserted by early editors are omitted (as has become standard practice), but for the convenience of those who miss them, an indication of locale now appears as the first item in the annotation of each scene.

In the interest of both elegance and utility, each speech prefix is set in a separate line when the speakers' lines are in verse, except when those words form the second half of a verse line. Thus the verse form of the speech is kept visually intact. What is printed as verse and what is printed as prose has, in general, the authority of the original texts. Departures from the original texts in this regard have the authority only of editorial tradition and the judgment of the Pelican editors; and, in a few instances, are admittedly arbitrary.

The Theatrical World

Economic REALITIES determined the theatrical world in which Shakespeare's plays were written, performed, and received. For centuries in England, the primary theatrical tradition was nonprofessional. Craft guilds (or "mysteries") provided religious drama – mystery plays – as part of the celebration of religious and civic festivals, and schools and universities staged classical and neoclassical drama in both Latin and English as part of their curricula. In these forms, drama was established and socially acceptable. Professional theater, in contrast, existed on the margins of society. The acting companies were itinerant; playhouses could be any available space – the great halls of the aristocracy, town squares, civic halls, inn yards, fair booths, or open fields – and income was sporadic, dependent on the passing of the hat or on the bounty of local patrons. The actors, moreover, were considered little better than vagabonds, constantly in danger of arrest or expulsion.

In the late 1560s and 1570s, however, English professional theater began to gain respectability. Wealthy aristocrats fond of drama – the Lord Admiral, for example, or the Lord Chamberlain – took acting companies under their protection so that the players technically became members of their households and were no longer subject to arrest as homeless or masterless men. Permanent theaters were first built at this time as well, allowing the companies to control and charge for entry to their performances.

Shakespeare's livelihood, and the stunning artistic explosion in which he participated, depended on pragmatic and architectural effort. Professional theater requires ways to restrict access to its offerings; if it does not, and admission fees cannot be charged, the actors do not get paid, the costumes go to a pawnbroker, and there is no such thing as a professional, ongoing theatrical tradition. The answer to that economic need arrived in the late 1560s and 1570s with the creation of the so-called public or amphitheater playhouse. Recent discoveries indicate that the precursor of the Globe playhouse in London (where Shakespeare's mature plays were presented) and the Rose theater (which presented Christopher Marlowe's plays and some of Shakespeare's earliest ones) was the Red Lion theater of 1567. Archaeological studies of the foundations of the Rose and Globe theaters have revealed that the open-air theater of the 1590s and later was probably a polygonal building with fourteen to twenty or twenty-four sides, multistoried, from 75 to 100 feet in diameter, with a raised, partly covered "thrust" stage that projected into a group of standing patrons, or "groundlings," and a covered gallery, seating up to 2,500 or more (very crowded) spectators.

These theaters might have been about half full on any given day, though the audiences were larger on holidays or when a play was advertised, as old and new were, through printed playbills posted around London. The metropolitan area's late-Tudor, early-Stuart population (circa 1590–1620) has been estimated at about 150,000–250,000. It has been supposed that in the mid-1590s there were about 15,000 spectators per week at the public theaters; thus, as many as 10 percent of the local population went to the theater regularly. Consequently, the theaters' repertories – the plays available for this experienced and frequent audience – had to change often: in the month between September 15 and October 15, 1595, for instance, the Lord Admiral's Men performed twenty-eight times in eighteen different plays.

Since natural light illuminated the amphitheaters' stages, performances began between noon and two o'clock and ran without a break for two or three hours. They often concluded with a jig, a fencing display, or some other nondramatic exhibition. Weather conditions determined the season for the amphitheaters: plays were performed every day (including Sundays, sometimes, to clerical dismay) except during Lent – the forty days before Easter – or periods of plague, or sometimes during the summer months when law courts were not in session and the most affluent members of the audience were not in London.

To a modern theatergoer, an amphitheater stage like that of the Rose or Globe would appear an unfamiliar mixture of plainness and elaborate decoration. Much of the structure was carved or painted, sometimes to imitate marble; elsewhere, as under the canopy projecting over the stage, to represent the stars and the zodiac. Appropriate painted canvas pictures (of Jerusalem, for example, if the play was set in that city) were apparently hung on the wall behind the acting area, and tragedies were accompanied by black hangings, presumably something like crepe festoons or bunting. Although these theaters did not employ what we would call scenery, early modern spectators saw numerous large props, such as the "bar" at which a prisoner stood during a trial, the "mossy bank" where lovers reclined, an arbor for amorous conversation, a chariot, gallows, tables, trees, beds, thrones, writing desks, and so forth. Audiences might learn a scene's location from a sign (reading "Athens," for example) carried across the stage (as in Bertolt Brecht's twentieth-century productions). Equally captivating (and equally irritating to the theater's enemies) were the rich costumes and personal props the actors used: the most valuable items in the surviving theatrical inventories are the swords, gowns, robes, crowns, and other items worn or carried by the performers.

Magic appealed to Shakespeare's audiences as much as it does to us today, and the theater exploited many deceptive and spectacular devices. A winch in the loft above the stage, called "the heavens," could lower and raise actors playing gods, goddesses, and other supernatural figures to and from the main acting area, just as one or more trapdoors permitted entrances and exits to and from the area, called "hell," beneath the stage. Actors wore elementary makeup such as wigs, false beards, and face paint, and they employed pigs' bladders filled with animal blood to make wounds seem more real. They had rudimentary but effective ways of pretending to behead or hang a person. Supernumeraries (stagehands or actors not needed in a particular scene) could make thunder sounds (by shaking a metal sheet or rolling an iron ball down a chute) and show lightning (by blowing inflammable resin through tubes into a flame). Elaborate fireworks enhanced the effects of dragons flying through the air or imitated such celestial phenomena as comets, shooting stars, and multiple suns. Horses' hoofbeats, bells (located perhaps in the tower above the stage), trumpets and drums, clocks, cannon shots and gunshots, and the like were common sound effects. And the music of viols, cornets, oboes, and recorders was a regular feature of theatrical performances.

For two relatively brief spans, from the late 1570s to 1590 and from 1599 to 1614, the amphitheaters competed with the so-called private, or indoor, theaters, which originated as, or later represented themselves as, educational institutions training boys as singers for church services and court performances. These indoor theaters had two features that were distinct from the amphitheaters': their personnel and their playing spaces. The amphitheaters' adult companies included both adult men, who played the male roles, and boys, who played the female roles; the private, or indoor, theater companies, on the other hand, were entirely composed of boys aged about 8 to 16, who were, or could pretend to be, candidates for singers in a church or a royal boys' choir. (Until 1660, professional theatrical companies included no women.) The playing space would appear much more familiar to modern audiences than the long-vanished amphitheaters; the later indoor theaters were, in fact, the ancestors of the typical modern theater. They were enclosed spaces, usually rectangular, with the stage filling one end of the rectangle and the audience arrayed in seats or benches across (and sometimes lining) the building's longer axis. These spaces staged plays less frequently than the public theaters (perhaps only once a week) and held far fewer spectators than the amphitheaters: about 200 to 600, as opposed to 2,500 or more. Fewer patrons mean a smaller gross income, unless each pays more. Not surprisingly, then, private theaters charged higher prices than the amphitheaters, probably sixpence, as opposed to a penny for the cheapest entry.

Protected from the weather, the indoor theaters presented plays later in the day than the amphitheaters, and used artificial illumination – candles in sconces or candelabra. But candles melt, and need replacing, snuffing, and trimming, and these practical requirements may have been part of the reason the indoor theaters introduced breaks in the performance, the intermission so dear to the heart of theatergoers and to the pocketbooks of theater concessionaires ever since. Whether motivated by the need to tend to the candles or by the entrepreneurs' wishing to sell oranges and liquor, or both, the indoor theaters eventually established the modern convention of the non-continuous performance. In the early modern "private" theater, musical performances apparently filled the intermissions, which in Stuart theater jargon seem to have been called "acts."

At the end of the first decade of the seventeenth century, the distinction between public amphitheaters and private indoor companies ceased. For various cultural, political, and economic reasons, individual companies gained control of both the public, open-air theaters and the indoor ones, and companies mixing adult men and boys took over the formerly "private" theaters. Despite the death of the boys' companies and of their highly innovative theaters (for which such luminous playwrights as Ben Jonson, George Chapman, and John Marston wrote), their playing spaces and conventions had an immense impact on subsequent plays: not merely for the intervals (which stressed the artistic and architectonic importance of "acts"), but also because they introduced political and social satire as a popular dramatic ingredient, even in tragedy, and a wider range of actorly effects, encouraged by their more intimate playing spaces.

Even the briefest sketch of the Shakespearean theatrical world would be incomplete without some comment on the social and cultural dimensions of theaters and playing in the period. In an intensely hierarchical and status-conscious society, professional actors and their ventures had hardly any respectability; as we have indicated, to protect themselves against laws designed to curb vagabondage and the increase of masterless men, actors resorted to the near-fiction that they were the servants of noble masters, and wore their distinctive livery. Hence the company for which Shakespeare wrote in the 1590s that called itself the Lord Chamberlain's Men and pretended that the public, money-getting performances were in fact rehearsals for private performances before that high court official. From 1598, the Privy Council had licensed theatrical companies, and after 1603, with the accession of King James I, the companies gained explicit royal protection, just as the Queen's Men had for a time under Queen Elizabeth. The Chamberlain's Men became the King's Men, and the other companies were patronized by the other members of the royal family.

These designations were legal fictions that half-concealed an important economic and social development, the evolution away from the theater's organization on the model of the guild, a self-regulating confraternity of individual artisans, into a proto-capitalist organization. Shakespeare's company became a joint-stock company, where persons who supplied capital and, in some cases, such as Shakespeare's, capital and talent, employed themselves and others in earning a return on that capital. This development meant that actors and theater companies were outside both the traditional guild structures, which required some form of civic or royal charter, and the feudal household organization of master-and-servant. This anomalous, maverick social and economic condition made theater companies practically unruly and potentially even dangerous; consequently, numerous official bodies – including the London metropolitan and ecclesiastical authorities as well as, occasionally, the royal court itself – tried, without much success, to control and even to disband them.

Public officials had good reason to want to close the theaters: they were attractive nuisances – they drew often riotous crowds, they were always noisy, and they could be politically offensive and socially insubordinate. Until the Civil War, however, anti-theatrical forces failed to shut down professional theater, for many reasons – limited surveillance and few police powers, tensions or outright hostilities among the agencies that sought to check or channel theatrical activity, and lack of clear policies for control. Another reason must have been the theaters' undeniable popularity. Curtailing any activity enjoyed by such a substantial percentage of the population was difficult, as various Roman emperors attempting to limit circuses had learned, and the Tudor-Stuart audience was not merely large, it was socially diverse and included women. The prevalence of public entertainment in this period has been underestimated. In fact, fairs, holidays, games, sporting events, the equivalent of modern parades, freak shows, and street exhibitions all abounded, but the theater was the most widely and frequently available entertainment to which people of every class had access. That fact helps account both for its quantity and for the fear and anger it aroused.

Books About Shakespeare's Theater

Useful scholarly studies of theatrical life in Shakespeare's day include: G. E. Bentley, *The Jacobean and Caroline Stage*, 7 vols. (1941–68), and the same author's *The Professions of Dramatist and Player in Shakespeare's Time, 1590–1642* (1986); Julian Bowsher, *The Rose Theatre: An Archaeological Discovery* (1998); E. K. Chambers, *The Elizabethan Stage*, 4 vols. (1923); Christine Eccles, *The Rose*

Theatre (1990); R. A. Foakes, *Illustrations of the English Stage, 1580–1642* (1985); Andrew Gurr, *The Shakespearean Stage, 1574–1642*, 3rd ed. (1992), and the same author's *Playgoing in Shakespeare's London*, 2nd ed. (1996); Roslyn Lander Knutson, *Playing Companies and Commerce in Shakespeare's Time* (2001); Edwin Nungezer, *A Dictionary of Actors* (1929); Carol Chillington Rutter, ed., *Documents of the Rose Playhouse* (1984); Tiffany Stern, *Documents of Performance in Early Modern England* (2009); Glynne Wickham, Herbert Berry, and William Ingram, *English Professional Theatre, 1530–1660* (2009).

WILLIAM SHAKESPEARE OF STRATFORD-UPON-AVON, GENTLEMAN

Many people have said that we know very little about William Shakespeare's life – pinheads and postcards are often mentioned as appropriately tiny surfaces on which to record the available information. More imaginatively and perhaps more correctly, Ralph Waldo Emerson wrote, "Shakespeare is the only biographer of Shakespeare. . . . So far from Shakespeare's being the least known, he is the one person in all modern history fully known to us."

In fact, we know more about Shakespeare's life than we do about almost any other English writer's of his era. His last will and testament (dated March 25, 1616) survives, as do numerous legal contracts and court documents involving Shakespeare as principal or witness, and parish records in Stratford and London. Shakespeare appears quite often in official records of King James's royal court, and of course Shakespeare's name appears on numerous title pages and in the written and recorded words of his literary contemporaries Robert Greene, Henry Chettle, Francis Meres, John Davies of Hereford, Ben Jonson, and many others. Indeed, if we make due allowance for the bloating of modern, run-of-the-mill bureaucratic records, more information has survived over the past four hundred years about William Shakespeare of Stratford-upon-Avon, Warwickshire, than is likely to survive in the next four hundred years about any reader of these words.

What we do not have are entire categories of information – Shakespeare's private letters or diaries, drafts and revisions of poems and plays, critical prefaces or essays, commendatory verse for other writers' works, or instructions guiding his fellow actors in their performances, for instance – that we imagine would help us understand and appreciate his surviving writings. For all we know, many such data never existed as written records. Many literary and theatrical critics, not knowing what might once have existed, more or less cheerfully accept the situation; some even make a theoretical virtue of it by claiming that such data are irrelevant to understanding and interpreting the plays and poems.

So, what do we know about William Shakespeare, the man responsible for thirty-seven or perhaps more plays, more than 150 sonnets, two lengthy narrative poems, and some shorter poems?

While many families by the name of Shakespeare (or some variant spelling) can be identified in the English Midlands as far back as the twelfth century, it seems likely that the dramatist's grandfather, Richard, moved to Snitterfield, a town not far from Stratford-upon-Avon, sometime before 1529. In Snitterfield, Richard Shakespeare leased farmland from the very wealthy Robert Arden. By 1552, Richard's son John had moved to a large house on Henley Street in Stratford-upon-Avon, the house that stands today as "The Birthplace." In Stratford, John Shakespeare traded as a glover, dealt in wool, and lent money at interest; he also served in a variety of civic posts, including "High Bailiff," the municipality's equivalent of mayor. In 1557, he married Robert Arden's youngest daughter, Mary. Mary and John had four sons – William was the oldest – and four daughters, of whom only Joan outlived her most celebrated sibling. William was baptized (an event entered in the Stratford parish church records) on April 26, 1564, and it has become customary, without any good factual support, to suppose he was born on April 23, which happens to be the feast day of Saint George, patron saint of England, and is also the date on which he died, in 1616. Shakespeare married Anne Hathaway in 1582, when he was eighteen and she was twenty-six; their first child was born five months later. It has been generally assumed that the marriage was enforced and subsequently unhappy, but these are only assumptions; it has been estimated, for instance, that up to one third of Elizabethan brides were pregnant when they married. Anne and William Shakespeare had three children: Susanna, who married a prominent local physician, John Hall; and the twins Hamnet, who died young in 1596, and Judith, who married Thomas Quiney – apparently a rather shady individual. The name Hamnet was unusual but not unique: he and his twin sister were named for their godparents, Shakespeare's neighbors Hamnet and Judith Sadler. Shakespeare's father died in 1601 (the year of *Hamlet*), and Mary Arden Shakespeare died in 1608 (the year of *Coriolanus*). William Shakespeare's last surviving direct descendant was his granddaughter Elizabeth Hall, who died in 1670.

Between the birth of the twins in 1585 and a clear reference to Shakespeare as a practicing London dramatist in Robert Greene's sensationalizing, satiric pamphlet, *Greene's Groatsworth of Wit* (1592), there is no record of where William Shakespeare was or what he was doing. These seven so-called lost years have been imaginatively filled by scholars and other students of Shakespeare: some think he traveled to Italy, or fought in the Low Countries, or studied law or medicine, or worked as an apprentice actor/writer, and so on to even more fanciful possibilities. Whatever the biographical facts for those "lost" years, Greene's nasty remarks in 1592 testify to professional envy and to the fact that Shakespeare already had a successful career in London. Speaking to his fellow playwrights, Greene warns both generally and specifically:

... trust them [actors] not: for there is an upstart crow, beautified with our feathers, that with his tiger's heart wrapped in a player's hide supposes he is as well able to bombast out a blank verse as the best of you; and being an absolute Johannes Factotum, is in his own conceit the only Shake-scene in a country.

The passage mimics a line from *3 Henry VI* (hence the play must have been performed before Greene wrote) and seems to say that "Shake-scene" is both actor and playwright, a jack-of-all-trades. That same year, Henry Chettle protested Greene's remarks in *Kind-Heart's Dream*, and each of the next two years saw the publication of poems – *Venus and Adonis* and *The Rape of Lucrece*, respectively – publicly ascribed to (and dedicated by) Shakespeare. Early in 1595 he was named one of the senior members of a prominent acting company, the Lord Chamberlain's Men, when they received payment for court performances during the 1594 Christmas season.

Clearly, Shakespeare had achieved both success and reputation in London. In 1596, upon Shakespeare's application, the College of Arms granted his father the now-familiar coat of arms he had taken the first steps to obtain almost twenty years before, and in 1598, John's son – now permitted to call himself "gentleman" – took a 10 percent share in the new Globe playhouse. In 1597, he bought a substantial bourgeois house, called New Place, in Stratford – the garden remains, but Shakespeare's house, several times rebuilt, was torn down in 1759 – and over the next few years Shakespeare spent large sums buying land and making other investments in the town and its environs. Though he worked in London, his family remained in Stratford, and he seems always to have considered Stratford the home he would eventually return to. Something approaching a disinterested appreciation of Shakespeare's popular and professional status appears in Francis Meres's *Palladis Tamia* (1598), a not especially imaginative and perhaps therefore persuasive record of lit-

erary reputations. Reviewing contemporary English writ-
ers, Meres lists the titles of many of Shakespeare's plays,
including one not now known, *Love's Labor's Won,* and
praises his "mellifluous & hony-tongued" "sugred Son-
nets," which were then circulating in manuscript (they
were first collected in 1609). Meres describes Shakespeare
as "one of the best" English playwrights of both comedy
and tragedy. In *Remains . . . Concerning Britain* (1605),
William Camden – a more authoritative source than the
imitative Meres – calls Shakespeare one of the "most
pregnant witts of these our times" and joins him with
such writers as Chapman, Daniel, Jonson, Marston, and
Spenser. During the first decades of the seventeenth cen-
tury, publishers began to attribute numerous play quartos,
including some non-Shakespearean ones, to Shakespeare,
either by name or initials, and we may assume that they
deemed Shakespeare's name and supposed authorship,
true or false, commercially attractive.

For the next ten years or so, various records show
Shakespeare's dual career as playwright and man of the
theater in London, and as an important local figure in
Stratford. In 1608-9 his acting company – designated
the "King's Men" soon after King James had succeeded
Queen Elizabeth in 1603 – rented, refurbished, and
opened a small interior playing space, the Blackfriars the-
ater, in London, and Shakespeare was once again listed as a
substantial sharer in the group of proprietors of the play-
house. By May 11, 1612, however, he describes himself as
a Stratford resident in a London lawsuit – an indication
that he had withdrawn from day-to-day professional ac-
tivity and returned to the town where he had always had
his main financial interests. When Shakespeare bought a
substantial residential building in London, the Blackfriars
Gatehouse, close to the theater of the same name, on
March 10, 1613, he is recorded as William Shakespeare
"of Stratford upon Avon in the county of Warwick, gen-
tleman," and he named several London residents as the
building's trustees. Still, he continued to participate in

theatrical activity: when the new Earl of Rutland needed an allegorical design to bear as a shield, or *impresa,* at the celebration of King James's Accession Day, March 24, 1613, the earl's accountant recorded a payment of 44 shillings to Shakespeare for the device with its motto.

For the last few years of his life, Shakespeare evidently concentrated his activities in the town of his birth. Most of the final records concern business transactions in Stratford, ending with the notation of his death on April 23, 1616, and burial in Holy Trinity Church, Stratford-upon-Avon.

THE QUESTION OF AUTHORSHIP

The history of ascribing Shakespeare's plays (the poems do not come up so often) to someone else began, as it continues, peculiarly. The earliest published claim that someone else wrote Shakespeare's plays appeared in an 1856 article by Delia Bacon in the American journal *Putnam's Monthly* – although an Englishman, Thomas Wilmot, had shared his doubts in private (even secretive) conversations with friends near the end of the eighteenth century. Bacon's was a sad personal history that ended in madness and poverty, but the year after her article, she published, with great difficulty and the bemused assistance of Nathaniel Hawthorne (then United States Consul in Liverpool, England), her *Philosophy of the Plays of Shakspere Unfolded.* This huge, ornately written, confusing farrago is almost unreadable; sometimes its intents, to say nothing of its arguments, disappear entirely beneath near-raving, ecstatic writing. Tumbled in with much supposed "philosophy" appear the claims that Francis Bacon (from whom Delia Bacon eventually claimed descent), Walter Raleigh, and several other contemporaries of Shakespeare's had written the plays. The book had little impact except as a ridiculed curiosity.

Once proposed, however, the issue gained momentum

among people whose conviction was the greater in proportion to their ignorance of sixteenth- and seventeenth-century English literature, history, and society. Another American amateur, Catharine F. Ashmead Windle, made the next influential contribution to the cause when she published *Report to the British Museum* (1882), wherein she promised to open "the Cipher of Francis Bacon," though what she mostly offers, in the words of S. Schoenbaum, is "demented allegorizing." An entire new cottage industry grew from Windle's suggestion that the texts contain hidden, cryptographically discoverable ciphers – "clues" – to their authorship; and today there are not only books devoted to the putative ciphers, but also pamphlets, journals, and newsletters.

Although Baconians have led the pack of those seeking a substitute Shakespeare, in *"Shakespeare" Identified* (1920), J. Thomas Looney became the first published "Oxfordian" when he proposed Edward de Vere, seventeenth earl of Oxford, as the secret author of Shakespeare's plays. Also for Oxford and his "authorship" there are today dedicated societies, articles, journals, and books. Less popular candidates – Queen Elizabeth and Christopher Marlowe among them – have had adherents, but the movement seems to have divided into two main contending factions, Baconian and Oxfordian. (For further details on all the candidates for "Shakespeare," see S. Schoenbaum, *Shakespeare's Lives,* 2nd ed., 1991.)

The Baconians, the Oxfordians, and supporters of other candidates have one trait in common – they are snobs. Every pro-Bacon or pro-Oxford tract sooner or later claims that the historical William Shakespeare of Stratford-upon-Avon could not have written the plays because he could not have had the training, the university education, the experience, and indeed the imagination or background their author supposedly possessed. Only a learned genius like Bacon or an aristocrat like Oxford could have written such fine plays. (As it happens, lucky male children of the middle class had access to better education than most aristocrats in Elizabethan England – and Oxford was not particularly well educated.) Shakespeare received in the Stratford grammar school a formal education that would daunt many college graduates today; and popular rival playwrights such as the very learned Ben Jonson and George Chapman, both of whom also lacked university training, achieved great artistic success, without being taken as Bacon or Oxford.

Besides snobbery, one other quality characterizes the authorship controversy: lack of evidence. A great deal of testimony from Shakespeare's time shows that Shakespeare wrote Shakespeare's plays and that his contemporaries recognized them as distinctive and distinctly superior. (Some of that contemporary evidence is collected in E. K. Chambers, *William Shakespeare: A Study of Facts and Problems,* 2 vols., 1930.) Since that testimony comes from Shakespeare's enemies and theatrical competitors as well as from his co-workers and from the Elizabethan equivalent of literary journalists, it seems unlikely that, if any one of these sources had known he was a fraud, they would have failed to record that fact.

Books About Shakespeare's Life

The following books provide scholarly, documented accounts of Shakespeare's life: G. E. Bentley, *Shakespeare: A Biographical Handbook* (1961); E. K. Chambers, *William Shakespeare: A Study of Facts and Problems,* 2 vols. (1930); S. Schoenbaum, *William Shakespeare: A Compact Documentary Life* (1977), and the same author's *Shakespeare's Lives,* 2nd ed. (1991); James Shapiro, *Contested Will: Who Wrote Shakespeare?* (2010). Many scholarly editions of Shakespeare's complete works print brief compilations of essential dates and events. References to Shakespeare's works up to 1700 are collected in C. M. Ingleby et al., *Shakespeare Allusion-Book,* rev. ed., 2 vols. (1932).

The Texts of Shakespeare

As FAR AS WE KNOW, only one manuscript conceivably in Shakespeare's own hand may (and even this is much disputed) exist: a few pages of a play called *Sir Thomas More*, which apparently was never performed. What we do have, as later readers, performers, scholars, students, are printed texts. The earliest of these survive in two forms: quartos and folios. Quartos (from the Latin for "four") are small books, printed on sheets of paper that were then folded twice, to make four leaves or eight pages. When these were bound together, the result was a squarish, eminently portable volume that sold for the relatively small sum of sixpence (translating in modern terms to about $5). In folios, on the other hand, the sheets are folded only once, in half, producing large, impressive volumes taller than they are wide. This was the format for important works of philosophy, science, theology, and literature (the major precedent for a folio Shakespeare was Ben Jonson's *Works*, 1616). The decision to print the works of a popular playwright in folio is an indication of how far up on the social scale the theatrical profession had come during Shakespeare's lifetime. The Shakespeare folio was an expensive book, selling for between fifteen and eighteen shillings, depending on the binding (in modern terms, from about $150 to $180). Twenty Shakespeare plays of the thirty-seven that survive first appeared in quarto, seventeen of which appeared during Shakespeare's lifetime; the rest of the plays are found only in folio.

The First Folio was published in 1623, seven years after Shakespeare's death, and was authorized by his fellow actors, the co-owners of the King's Men. This publication was certainly a mark of the company's enormous respect for Shakespeare; but it was also a way of turning the old plays, most of which were no longer current in the play-house, into ready money (the folio includes only Shakespeare's plays, not his sonnets or other nondramatic verse). Whatever the motives behind the publication of the folio, the texts it preserves constitute the basis for almost all later editions of the playwright's works. The texts, however, differ from those of the earlier quartos, sometimes in minor respects but often significantly – most strikingly in the two texts of *King Lear,* but also in important ways in *Hamlet, Othello,* and *Troilus and Cressida.* (The variants are recorded in the textual notes to each play in the new Pelican series.) The differences in these texts represent, in a sense, the essence of theater: the texts of plays were initially not intended for publication. They were scripts, designed for the actors to perform – the principal life of the play at this period was in performance. And it follows that in Shakespeare's theater the playwright typically had no say either in how his play was performed or in the disposition of his text – he was an employee of the company. The authoritative figures in the theatrical enterprise were the shareholders in the company, who were for the most part the major actors. They decided what plays were to be done; they hired the playwright and often gave him an outline of the play they wanted him to write. Often, too, the play was a collaboration: the company would retain a group of writers, and parcel out the scenes among them. The resulting script was then the property of the company, and the actors would revise it as they saw fit during the course of putting it on stage. The resulting text belonged to the company. The playwright had no rights in it once he had been paid. (This system survives largely intact in the movie industry, and most of the playwrights of Shakespeare's time were as anonymous as most screenwriters are today.) The script could also, of course, continue to change as the tastes of audiences and the requirements of the actors changed. Many – perhaps most – plays were revised when they were reintroduced after any substantial absence from the repertory, or when they were performed by a company different from the one that originally commissioned the play.

Shakespeare was an exceptional figure in this world because he was not only a shareholder and actor in his company, but also its leading playwright – he was literally his own boss. He had, moreover, little interest in the publication of his plays, and even those that appeared during his lifetime with the authorization of the company show no signs of any editorial concern on the part of the author. Theater was, for Shakespeare, a fluid and supremely responsive medium – the very opposite of the great classic canonical text that has embodied his works since 1623.

The very fluidity of the original texts, however, has meant that Shakespeare has always had to be edited. Here is an example of how problematic the editorial project inevitably is, a passage from the most famous speech in *Romeo and Juliet,* Juliet's balcony soliloquy beginning "O Romeo, Romeo, wherefore art thou Romeo?" Since the eighteenth century, the standard modern text has read,

> What's Montague? It is nor hand, nor foot,
> Nor arm, nor face, nor any other part
> Belonging to a man. O be some other name!
> What's in a name? That which we call a rose
> By any other name would smell as sweet.
> (II.2.40–44)

Editors have three early texts of this play to work from, two quarto texts and the folio. Here is how the First Quarto (1597) reads:

> Whats *Mountague?* It is nor hand nor foote,
> Nor arme, nor face, nor any other part.
> Whats in a name? That which we call a Rofe,
> By any other name would fmell as fweet:

Here is the Second Quarto (1599):

> Whats *Mountague* ? it is nor hand nor foote,
> Nor arme nor face, ô be some other name
> Belonging to a man.
> Whats in a name that which we call a rose,
> By any other word would smell as sweete,

And here is the First Folio (1623):

> What's *Mountague* ? it is nor hand nor foote,
> Nor arme, nor face, O be some other name
> Belonging to a man.
> What ? in a names that which we call a Rose,
> By any other word would smell as sweete,

There is in fact no early text that reads as our modern text does – and this is the most famous speech in the play. Instead, we have three quite different texts, all of which are clearly some version of the same speech, but none of which seems to us a final or satisfactory version. The transcendently beautiful passage in modern editions is an editorial invention: editors have succeeded in conflating and revising the three versions into something we recognize as great poetry. Is this what Shakespeare "really" wrote? Who can say? What we can say is that Shakespeare always had performance, not a book, in mind.

Books About the Shakespeare Texts

The standard study of the printing history of the First Folio is W. W. Greg, *The Shakespeare First Folio* (1955). J. K. Walton, *The Quarto Copy for the First Folio of Shakespeare* (1971), is a useful survey of the relation of the quartos to the folio. The second edition of Charlton Hinman's *Norton Facsimile* of the First Folio (1996), with a new introduction by Peter Blayney, is indispensable. Stanley Wells and Gary Taylor, *William Shakespeare: A Textual Companion,* keyed to the Oxford text, gives a comprehensive survey of the editorial situation for all the plays and poems.

Introduction

Authorship and Selection of Poems

THE POEMS INCLUDED in any volume of Shakespeare's poetry will vary according to current scholarly beliefs about which poems Shakespeare actually wrote. These beliefs have changed over time, and the poems included have varied accordingly. This edition is not one in which a full scholarly review of authorship can be undertaken, although I outline below some of the relevant current issues regarding authorship and attribution of the poems. My editorial choices are conservative by present-day standards, yet their being so has more to do with the scope of this edition than with opposition to recent, radical trends in Shakespeare editing.

The main works in this section are Shakespeare's long narrative poems, *Venus and Adonis* and *Lucrece*, retitled *The Rape of Lucrece* in the sixth quarto edition of 1616. *The Phoenix and the Turtle* is included; so are poems from a 1599 lyric collection called *The Passionate Pilgrim*, on the title page of which Shakespeare is named as the author. I have included *A Lover's Complaint* for the same reason. Although Shakespeare's authorship of the poem remains doubtful, it was published under his name in the 1609 edition of the sonnets. *Venus and Adonis, Lucrece*, and *The Phoenix and the Turtle* are self-selecting, since their status as poems written by Shakespeare cannot seriously be challenged in our present state of knowledge. On the other hand, *The Passionate Pilgrim*, first published in 1599 by the entrepreneurial printer William Jaggard, includes versions of poems by Shakespeare that are known from other sources, yet it also includes poems by other contemporary poets, and poems of unknown authorship, some of these included in other volumes as well. In 1612, Jaggard reprinted the volume and expanded it by adding nine poems by Thomas Heywood. Heywood objected, making the disarming complaint that his poems were unworthy to be published under Shakespeare's name. A new title page was therefore produced without Shakespeare's name on it. Because the volume initially appeared under Shakespeare's name, however, all the attested poems by Shakespeare plus those of undetermined authorship are included here, even though some of the latter cannot credibly be assigned to Shakespeare.

With the exception of the unassigned poems in *The Passionate Pilgrim*, and *A Lover's Complaint*, no poems doubtfully attributed to Shakespeare by previous scholars appear in this edition. This decision may seem conservative because Shakespeare editors are now generally reluctant to draw a hard line between what is authentically Shakespearean and what is not. At a theoretical level, claiming exclusive authorship on behalf of Shakespeare (or any of his contemporaries) has been challenged as both misguided and anachronistic. It is misguided because it credits the author, whether Shakespeare or anyone else, with a godlike power and control over the text never attainable under any conditions of literary production. It is anachronistic because it projects a modern conception (indeed, a modern fetish) of sole authorship back into Shakespeare's period, when collaborative production was not uncommon. What is certain is that compositors and printers contributed even to the texts we most confidently attribute to Shakespeare, as did actors in the case of the plays. It is not just the authorship of particular texts but *exclusive* authorship that remains "doubtful" in connection with Shakespeare and his contemporaries.

Practical as well as theoretical difficulties confront any attempt to determine exactly what belongs to Shakespeare and what does not. In many cases, Shakespeare's authorship is well established, yet in others – for example, the unassignable poems in *The Passionate Pilgrim*, and *A Lover's Complaint* – we simply can't be sure. Because they depend on historically shifting tastes, arguments based on poetic quality alone can never determine whether or not particular poems are by Shakespeare. We also have to admit that Shakespeare could have written bad or uncharacteristic poems. The fact that we think a poem bad or atypical does not necessarily mean that Shakespeare could not have written it.

Furthermore, in Shakespeare's time poems were often misattributed or dubiously attributed. To give one example of apparent misattribution (rather than just dubious attribution), a well-known manuscript assigns a poem called *Shall I Die?* to Shakespeare. Gary Taylor, coeditor of the Oxford Shakespeare, announced the poem as a newly discovered Shakespearean one in 1985. His claim gained widespread media attention in Britain and the United States before being broadly rejected by the scholarly community. After extensive discussion, it emerged that the poem was neither newly discovered nor convincingly attributable to Shakespeare.

In another case, a seventeenth-century poem in manuscript, titled *A Funeral Elegy* and signed W. S., was attributed to Shakespeare ("beyond all reasonable doubt") by Donald Foster in 1996, mainly on the basis of computer analysis. In this instance, principles of computer-assisted attribution were also on the line. Foster's claim gained some credence from his widely reported success in using computer analysis to identify Joe Klein as the author of an anonymously published novel called *Primary Colors,* a scandalous insider account of President Clinton's first election campaign.

Although many Shakespeareans initially credited Foster's claim on behalf of *A Funeral Elegy* (so much so that the poem was included at once in three new major editions of Shakespeare's complete works), that attribution has subsequently been challenged, also on the basis of computer analysis. Because of such uncertainties, and because appropriate tests to be used in computer attribution remain under development, both poems have been omitted here. So has a handful of epitaphs traditionally attributed to

Shakespeare. (*A Funeral Elegy,* deliberately omitted from the Pelican paperback edition of Shakespeare's *Narrative Poems,* has now convincingly been attributed to John Ford, not Shakespeare.)

One benefit arising from the need to include *The Passionate Pilgrim* is that it contains variant forms of poems published in the 1609 edition of Shakespeare's sonnets or in *Love's Labor's Lost. The Passionate Pilgrim,* like many of Shakespeare's plays, thus reminds us that what Shakespeare wrote seldom or never exists in any version that can be called final, definitive, or authoritative, even though a number of his poems and plays happen to have come down to us in only one version. As modern editors have increasingly come to believe, efforts to establish a single, definitive version are misdirected. In fact, countering the tendency of earlier editors to produce a single definitive text, modern editors have often found themselves de-editing Shakespeare. Their goal has been to restore his often multiple texts to something more like their condition during his lifetime, and up to the publication, seven years after his death, of the 1623 First Folio of the plays.

The Passionate Pilgrim also draws attention to the important role of lyric anthologies or "miscellanies" – even unauthorized ones – in circulating English poems during the sixteenth and seventeenth centuries. Many anthologies performed this function following Tottel's famous *Miscellany,* published in 1557, in which hitherto unprinted manuscript poems by Thomas Wyatt and Henry Howard, Earl of Surrey, were made widely available. A single narrative of the male lover's tribulations is sometimes implied in these collections of miscellaneous love poems, as it is in the 1609 volume of Shakespeare's sonnets. *The Passionate Pilgrim* also indicates that by 1599 it had become commercially advantageous for a publisher like Jaggard to exploit Shakespeare's name while producing a volume that included the work of others. *The Passionate Pilgrim* thus serves as an index of Shakespeare's poetic eminence and selling power by 1599, though his role, if any, in the production of the volume remains unknown. It additionally reveals the tendency of free-floating Renaissance lyrics to become attached to a successful poet's name, like iron filings to a magnet.

Venus and Adonis and *Lucrece*

Both *Venus and Adonis* and *Lucrece,* published respectively in 1593 and 1594, were highly successful (*Venus and Adonis* especially so) in the print market of Shakespeare's time. This fact made them suspect to at least some members of the educated elite. Shakespeare was mocked, for example, in the anonymous *Three Parnassus Plays* (1598-1602) for catering to low and possibly immoral public tastes; Parnassus, with which members of the academic community identified their universities, was the haunt of the Muses in classical literature. Thus the popularity of Shakespeare's poems, especially *Venus and Adonis,* retarded their academic acceptance as contemporary classics. Not all Shakespeare's contemporaries participated, however, in this snobbery. Printers and many leading writers as well as book buyers made no mistake about the power, brilliance, and cultural importance of Shakespeare's contribution. That recognition has only become more widespread, although its basis has continually shifted, down to our own time.

Much criticism has now been written about *Venus and Adonis* and *Lucrece* as important early works by Shakespeare, possibly composed while the London theaters were closed because of an outbreak of plague. Commentary on these poems has taken account of their literary-historical nature as variations on classical Latin themes; of their context of production under the patronage of the Earl of Southampton; of their appeal as widely read poems of their time; of their generic status as "minor epics"; of their rhetorical brilliance and showiness; of their conventional yet extraordinarily sophisticated reflection on relations between nature and art; and of their densely layered allusion to other texts and literary traditions. These are all important matters, repaying intensive study.

Instead of broadly surveying all these topics, however, I shall begin by focusing narrowly on the fact that both poems deal with what would now be regarded as forms of sexual violence or harassment. In *Venus and Adonis,* the powerful goddess of love pursues and sexually harasses an unwilling young man, while in *Lucrece,* one of Western history's best-known narratives of rape, originating in the Roman historian Livy's history of Rome, is retold and hugely amplified. In one story, the sexual aggressor is female while in the other the aggressor is male; in both cases, the victimized person dies. The thematic connection between the two poems is reinforced by a generic connection between them: both are so-called etiological poems. In other words, they are poems about how things originated, or got to be the way they are. In *Venus and Adonis,* the explicit question is how the tribulations of mortal lovers originated; in *Lucrece,* the implied question is how the modern politics of gender originated. How are we to understand Shakespeare's central preoccupation in these poems with sexuality, gender, and violence?

Before taking up this question, I should like to emphasize that Venus's harassment of Adonis and Tarquin the Younger's rape of Lucrece are not symmetrical. The rape of Lucrece is unequivocally understood to be criminal in the poem, whereas the courtship of Adonis by Venus is not. As a goddess, Venus is not subject to human law in any case. Correspondingly, the poems differ widely in tone and implication. The story of Venus and Adonis is told at an engagingly brisk pace, while the story of Lucrece often seems trapped in nightmarish immobility of a kind now often associated with representations of trauma. Despite the contrast, present-day readers may be struck by the focus of both poems on sexual (or sexualized) aggression.

Calling *Lucrece* a poem of sexual violence – or of sexualized violence – may seem like stating the obvious. It is worth recalling, however, that it took a succession of feminist critics, writing in the 1980s and '90s, to gain attention for the poem *as* one of sexual violence against a woman rather than, say, as a literary-historical, rhetorical, or aesthetic phenomenon only. Significant effort was needed, in other words, to focus attention on what the poem is about and to connect the story it tells to long-standing cultural patterns of gendered violence and abuse. Rape, in *Lucrece* and elsewhere, is no mere criminal exception but a revelation of pervasive gendered violence and inequality. That being so, it is no surprise that Shakespeare connects the rape of Lucrece to an extraordinarily wide range of causes and consequences. In fact, Shakespeare makes such connections on a scale unprecedented in retellings of the Lucrece story.

To call *Venus and Adonis* a poem of sexual violence might, in contrast, seem like stretching the point. Although Venus's pursuit of Adonis has been described as a rape in some earlier criticism, and although this pursuit is described in a 1994 psychological journal as an "early" representation of sexual harassment, these characterizations of the poem may seem either melodramatic or humorlessly clinical. The latter characterization may seem anachronistic as well. The criminalization of "harassment" is a recent and primarily North American phenomenon. Why then use the term in connection with Shakespeare's poem?

In *Venus and Adonis,* the story is told (often, it must be said, in entertainingly humorous fashion) of the goddess Venus's eager, lustful courtship of a young man named Adonis. Adonis consistently repels her advances, preferring to hunt with his male friends. Venus fears that he will be injured in this dangerous sport, and her worst fears are realized when he is killed by a wild boar, which gores him in the thigh. At his death, Adonis metamorphoses into a flower – unnamed by Shakespeare, but traditionally an anemone – and Venus retires to mourn in Paphos, prophesying that in the future mortals' love affairs will be unhappy and socially disruptive. The poem thus recounts the origin of lovers' endless trials.

This story, simple enough in its outline, is told by the Latin poet Ovid in his *Metamorphoses* and then retold by Shakespeare. In both Ovid and Shakespeare, Adonis undergoes metamorphosis into a flower. Here as elsewhere, the young Shakespeare is captivated by a fast-paced Ovidian story of love and suffering as well as by Ovid's sophisticated, witty, and often cheerfully heartless poetic style. The sheer exuberance and self-delight of Shakespeare's retelling of the story (a Shakespeare not just copying but outdoing Ovid) have been recognized by practically all critics of the poem. All of this seems a far cry from what we grimly call harassment. Yet a powerful metaphoric connection is made in the poem, ironically and unwittingly by Venus herself, between her uninhibited pursuit of Adonis and the injury he suffers from the boar:

> "'Tis true, 'tis true; thus was Adonis slain:
> He ran upon the boar with his sharp spear,
> Who did not whet his teeth at him again,
> But by a kiss thought to persuade him there;
> And nuzzling in his flank, the loving swine
> Sheathed unaware the tusk in his soft groin."
>
> (1111–16)

Perhaps Adonis's passion for the dangerous sport of hunting has represented a flight from Venus all along, into the relatively "safe" company of men. In any event, Shakespeare strongly implicates the goddess of love (or makes her implicate herself) in the death of her reluctant love object, even though she has begged him not to hunt. In fact, her affection is associated with the strange, ferocious, fatal "love" of the boar rather than simply opposed to it as protective concern. In the stanza quoted above, we arrive at the vanishing point of distinctions between human and animal, man and woman, sex and violence.

Additionally, the courtship of a bashful young man by Venus as an older woman implies the threat stereotypically experienced by young men of being overwhelmed by demanding, suffocating mother figures. The fact that Venus was represented as a mother, not just as the goddess of love, in classical literature adds this dimension of masculine anxiety to the pursuit of Adonis by Venus. The threatening importunity of the mother is written into this story of erotic courtship, as is masculine fear of quasi-incestuous maternal passion. Finally, the bizarre crisscrossing between Venus and the boar in the death of Adonis tends to make Venus what critical theorists have called the phallic mother, meaning the woman primordially invested with attributes of power ordinarily claimed by, or associated with, men. It is worth recalling here that Venus makes a terrifying appearance in *The Two Noble Kinsmen,* written at least in part by Shakespeare.

To imagine that a powerful older woman's persistent, coercive advances cannot count as damaging in Shakespeare's judgment (or be taken seriously even now as a form of sexual violence) is again to refuse consideration of what the poem is about. Refusing to take *Venus and Adonis* seriously may also entail the sexist assumption that while coercive or threatening advances by a man are serious, such advances by a woman, especially an older one, cannot be taken seriously, women being by definition powerless, so to speak, and their desires merely embarrassing. The idea that a woman might be capable of heterosexual rape is still foreign to our way of thinking, largely because the act of rape is so definitively associated with aggressive male penetration. Yet even if Shakespeare doesn't (or can't) make a tragedy of Adonis's death, he certainly associates Venus's advances with the fatal penetration of Adonis by the boar's tusk.

It is true that the woman in this case happens to be a goddess, not a human, thus giving a mythological and allegorical cast rather than a realistic one to the story. Although Elizabethans could read Ovid in Latin and in English translation, both his work and classical mythology in general were also relayed to the Elizabethans by vast, encyclopedic story collections with extensive allegorical commentaries. Reading pagan texts as allegories allowed Christian, mystical, or moral meanings to be extracted from them; this allegorical tendency was well established, and has been extensively studied in modern times. Yet the milieu in which Shakespeare wrote his poem was psychically dominated by a powerful, desiring woman in the person of Queen Elizabeth I. The threat as well as inspiration that she, along with some other powerful contemporary women like Mary Sidney, sister of Sir Philip Sidney, presented to male authors of her time has now been widely recognized. Shakespeare's complex response to the queen's presence is paralleled in the work of his great contemporary, Edmund Spenser, who also pointedly told the story of Venus and Adonis, in Book 3 of *The Faerie Queene*. It is no accident that throughout his career Shakespeare represented, in addition to the Venus of this poem, various powerful, desiring, sometimes charming, and often deadly women. To name only some: Titania (*A Midsummer Night's Dream*), Portia (*The Merchant of Venice*), Rosalind (*As You Like It*), Goneril and Regan (*King Lear*), Lady Macbeth (*Macbeth*), Volumnia (*Coriolanus*), Cleopatra (*Antony and Cleopatra*), and Paulina (*The Winter's Tale*).

We can fairly say, then, that at a certain level these two narrative poems represent two sides of the same coin. In making sex-power-gender relations central to both poems, Shakespeare strongly implies that those relations are culturally and politically fundamental. They are even made cosmically fundamental insofar as *Venus and Adonis* is a mythological poem about the power of love, personified by Venus; creative-destructive love can be seen as a cosmic force. Such mythological and cosmological treatment of the erotic, often inspired by Ovid, was extremely frequent in the work of Shakespeare and his contemporaries, among them Christopher Marlowe in *Hero and Leander*.

Personifying human passions in pagan gods and goddesses gave those passions a superhuman quality, beyond control. Deifying the passions further implied that the cruelly impersonal forces operating in the cosmos and determining individual human fates were primordial ones, not products of human culture. Procreative, heterosexual desire seems to be given the status of an amoral, universal force in

Shakespeare's poem when Venus's lust for Adonis is associ-
ated by way of a mock-epic simile with the lust of an eager
stallion: "He sees his love, and nothing else he sees, / For
nothing else with his proud sight agrees" (287–88). Ado-
nis's resistance to the cosmic energy of Venus's domain ac-
cordingly makes him seem deficient, childish, perverse,
non-procreative, and even doomed: he will neither yield to
Venus nor assume his proper role as a stallion – or as
Venus's "rider."

On the other hand, Adonis, who can hold his own in de-
bate, derides the speciousness of Venus's procreative argu-
ments. (The only "progeny" resulting from the relationship
is the flower Venus maternally cherishes in the end; since
flowers traditionally stand for poetic creations, the poem
becomes the sole "offspring" of this ill-fated love.) Further-
more, the status of aggressive heterosexual desire as an over-
riding natural imperative is set off in the poem against
forms of pain, flight, shrinking, withdrawal, and possibly
even male homoerotic resistance that seem no less natural.
(Parallels have been noted between the courtship of Adonis
in this poem and of the reluctant young man by an older
male speaker in Shakespeare's sonnets.) These natural sensi-
tivities are embodied in some of the poem's most affecting
comparisons – famous ones, for example, that sympatheti-
cally evoke the hunted hare's anguish or the snail's acute
sensitivity to injury:

> Or as the snail, whose tender horns being hit,
> Shrinks backward in his shelly cave with pain,
> And there all smothered up in shade doth sit,
> Long after fearing to creep forth again.
>
> (1033–36)

These sympathies are contradictorily embodied in Venus
herself, who is the subject of the snail comparison, and who
retires wounded, solitary, and grieving after the death of
Adonis. Thus, typically for works written in this period,
natural similes and analogies seem endlessly contradictory,

failing to resolve any ultimate questions and perpetually dividing sympathies. Both mythology and natural history provided a rich source of prototypes for reflection and poetic composition, but few resolutions. The intrusive narrative voice-over of *Venus and Adonis* oscillates between bright hardness and melting softness as the "natural" perspective shifts.

In *Venus and Adonis*, moreover, Shakespeare brings mythological and cosmological perspectives disconcertingly down to earth. Many modern readers, starting with the great critic C. S. Lewis, have been shocked at the mundane blowsiness of Venus in the poem. Shakespeare's Venus, who sweats, pants, invitingly falls on her back, and indecorously solicits sexual favors from an unwilling youth, is both a vulnerable and a somewhat shameful figure. The goddess of love is here made flesh; because she is so, it becomes possible both to sympathize with her predicament and feel queasy about her coercive pursuit of Adonis.

The field of the poem, then, is one of gendered inequality and sexual predation transmuted only to a degree by Venus's "humanity" and witty resourcefulness in courting Adonis. She amusingly yet ruthlessly exploits even his well-meaning concern for her when he thinks she has fainted:

> He chafes her lips, a thousand ways he seeks
> To mend the hurt that his unkindness marred;
> He kisses her, and she, by her good will,
> Will never rise, so he will kiss her still.
>
> (477–80)

Because of all this, the term "harassment" does not seem wholly out of place: unwanted witty persuasion may, after all, constitute harassment too, and "humorlessness" is a standard accusation against those who allege harassment. Yet in *Venus and Adonis* the harassment seems emblematic of a world in which power and desire are always unequally distributed. In a sense, everyone loses. Adonis dies, of course, even if he is metamorphosed into a pretty (poetic) flower as a result, while Venus cannot but alienate and participate in the destruction of the one she craves. Her divinity can save neither her nor Adonis. Part of the exhilaration of the poem, and of seeing Shakespeare exercising his phenomenal powers, comes from his brilliant retelling of a well-known story, but no less from his interest and involvement in the sexual politics of his world.

The same interest informs Shakespeare's *Lucrece,* now one of the most exhaustively discussed poems in the English language. Feminist attention to the poem must largely be given the credit for the intensiveness and high level of recent criticism, yet both the poem and the Lucrece story have been subjects of extremely wide-ranging scholarly investigation. Not only was the Lucrece story repeatedly retold from the time of Livy onwards, but Lucrece (or Lucretia) has often been painted. Among the images that have come down to us is a striking one by the Renaissance artist Artemisia Gentileschi, herself a victim of rape.

Lucrece suffers the anguish of rape and eventually commits suicide. Both the dynamics of rape and the predicament of the woman who has been raped have been at issue in much critical discussion, as they are in the poem. Shakespeare certainly gives unprecedented consideration to Lucrece's state of mind after the event. Yet, as I have already suggested, Shakespeare connects the rape of Lucrece not only to the politics of Rome but to an extensive historical and mythological vista, beginning with the fall of Troy. That story, told by Homer and Virgil among others, remained central to the European imagination from Greece through Rome down to the Renaissance.

When Lucrece tries to reorient herself after the rape, she studies a large painting (or tapestry) on which the siege of Troy by the Greeks is depicted. Readers will recall that the Trojan War began with the "rape" (in the inherited Latin sense of seizure or abduction) of Helen of Troy. A "rape" thus stands at the origin of Western epic, and what has been called "originary rape" thereby becomes the starting point in a story to which Romans connected their own imperial history through Virgil's epic poem the *Aeneid*. Indeed, originary rape seems to be repeated periodically: it is so in early Roman history when the Romans rape (abduct) the Sabine women to populate their new city. It is repeated again in the Lucrece story. Since the rapist is a member of the royal family, the rape of Lucrece becomes the crime that enables the Roman monarchy to be overthrown and a new republic to be instituted in its place. We witness this transition at the end of Shakespeare's poem, and it is a painful one insofar as Lucrece's suffering and death are speedily appropriated and forgotten by the men who dominate the Roman world, ambitiously plotting political change. Lucrece is used as the lever to dislodge the monarchy; her fate thus becomes merely instrumental. In short, not just gendered violence and inequality but also female sacrifice seem foundational for classical and postclassical European culture.

The connection between Troy (the rape of Helen) and Rome (the rape of Lucrece) becomes even more pointed when we recall that in Virgil's *Aeneid*, Rome's founding hero, Aeneas, is a Trojan who escapes from Troy before it falls to the Greeks. After many adventures, including his encounter with Dido, who is left to commit suicide after he abandons her, Aeneas lands in what is now Italy to become the founder of a new civilization. Troy is reborn as Rome. For the Roman Lucrece to look back to the Trojan origin is thus not surprising, nor is it surprising that she focuses on such female victims of Trojan history as Hecuba, the wife of King Priam, and Helen herself. Yet Lucrece dissociates herself from Helen, partly because Helen is suspect – portrayed as little better than a whore in Shakespeare's *Troilus and Cressida;* Lucrece also excoriates her: "Show me the strumpet that began this stir, / That with my nails her beauty I may tear" (1471-72). Long-standing cultural suspicions make it possible for Helen to be regarded as the passive-aggressive cause – exploiting her sexual power – and not the victim of the Trojan War. Whether as a result of misogynistic male suspicion or women's conniving, the discredited Helen cannot be the model for the innocent, raped woman.

It is rape, nevertheless, in Shakespeare's *Lucrece* and elsewhere that brings into the fullest possible view the systemic nature of unequal power-gender relations in Western culture. In a sense, the "powerful" woman operating within the system is the conniving one who can exploit these unequal relations rather than fall victim to them. The rape of Lucrece, however, brings into view the anguishing predicament – and powerlessness – of the innocent woman, just as it does the violent compulsions of the male rapist.

Sextus Tarquinius, the son of King Tarquin, does indeed rape Lucrece in Shakespeare's poem, although he knows full well that he is doing wrong, and foresees endless bad consequences for himself. Indeed, he agonizes over what he is doing and he finds afterwards that he has destroyed himself as well as Lucrece in the act. Ironically, it is his own feminine soul that he believes he has besmirched in raping Lucrece. If a certain sympathy is solicited for him as well as for Lucrece in the poem, that is partly because he seems driven by destructive social dynamisms he can neither understand nor resist, but partly too because, as rapist, he is acting within larger scenarios of gendered violence. Incriminating him alone thus makes him a scapegoat as well as a perpetrator. Even Lucrece, who has the best reason to blame him, cannot hold him wholly responsible, and she personifies abstractions like night, opportunity, and time after the rape in her quest of the ultimate perpetrator. The tragic rather than merely criminal potential of the Tarquin figure is recalled in Shakespeare's *Macbeth*, where Macbeth imagines himself as Tarquin in the moment when he goes forward to murder King Duncan.

Lucrece, on the other hand, represents the ideal of the chaste Roman wife, killing herself after her virtue has been tainted, even without her consent. She thus upholds core Roman values and survives in Roman cultural memory as an exemplary heroine. In expanding the narrative, however,

Shakespeare thoroughly complicates the picture and also questions the Roman heroic view of Lucrece. In the prose prologue to the poem, the Roman men are away from home, besieging the town of Ardea. They fall to boasting about their wives' faithfulness, and Collatine, Lucrece's husband, extols her virtue. Women's chastity as well as their beauty clearly confers status on their husbands; the chaste *beautiful* wife is supremely prized because, presumably, she is chaste by her own choice.

Wives also constitute a form of male property, making rape akin to theft or property damage suffered by the husband. In other words, the principal injury is done to the man rather than the woman. It becomes evident in the poem that Lucrece has been well schooled in these codes; the goods she feels to have been damaged after the rape are principally her husband's. It thus becomes extraordinarily difficult for her to process the rape subjectively – at first, she can hardly be said to have her own subjectivity – and reconcile herself to her new, damaged and devalued condition. Rather than just heroically exemplifying masculine Roman values, Lucrece in Shakespeare's poem becomes a figure through whom the harm done to women by Roman values and gender codes is critically exposed.

Shakespeare's critical eye is also trained on the way Collatine's boastful desire to "publish" his wife's virtue (a virtue that continues forever afterwards to be published, including by Shakespeare) invades her privacy and makes her sexual conquest the supreme challenge to other status-seeking men – for example, the king's son. Chastity itself becomes a powerful erotic-aggressive stimulus, perhaps the most powerful one of all. The publicity given to Lucrece by her husband thus exposes her to risk, and also invites intrusion into her private, domestic space. The very barriers to entry, including the legal prohibition on rape, serve as further limits to be boldly transgressed by the conqueror:

> This said, his guilty hand plucked up the latch,
> And with his knee the door he opens wide.

The dove sleeps fast that this night owl will catch;
Thus treason works ere traitors be espied.

(358-61)

Moreover, the publicity given to the chastely beautiful
wife, confined to the sphere of domestic privacy, incites in-
trusive and even pornographic fantasy: this intrusion be-
comes literal when Tarquin gazes at the exposed body of the
sleeping Lucrece: "Her breasts like ivory globes circled with
blue, / A pair of maiden worlds unconquerèd" (407-8). No
doubt this spectacle helped to make *Lucrece,* like *Venus and
Adonis,* into a popular erotic poem of its time, yet readers
may become aware that they are looking at Lucrece
through the eyes of the rapist. The "rape" of Lucrece is thus
occurring practically from the first moment of the poem
and forever after; it is an effect not just of male status rivalry
but of an entire social system that includes publication. So
much for ramifications.

To focus now more closely on Lucrece, let me recall that
Shakespeare's poem was initially published in 1594 under
the title *Lucrece,* before being retitled in 1616 as *The Rape
of Lucrece.* The latter title emphasizes the systemic violence
and extensive field of the *action* of rape. Retaining the orig-
inal title *Lucrece,* as I have done here, focuses attention
more fully on Lucrece as an isolated, exemplary sufferer
and heroine. It was in that guise that she most often ap-
peared in European paintings. As an icon, Lucrece could
become an object of sympathetic identification and admi-
ration, perhaps especially to women. Indeed, Lucrece was
assimilated, in postclassical literary history, into what the
English poet Geoffrey Chaucer called "the legend of good
women." She was thus removed, in effect, from the frame
of Roman masculinity and associated with other exemplary
women throughout history.

The peculiar anguish of Lucrece's situation, on which
Shakespeare dwells in the poem, is that of the innocent
woman who cannot fully believe in her own innocence or
escape an acute sense of shame. Innocent she may be, yet she

feels displaced from her social position and undermined in her integrity as a chaste married woman by the sexual violation she has suffered. Much of the verbal "excess" of the poem after the rape is generated by her inability to find a language in which to come to terms with her new situation: there is no fitting or expressive language for the raped Roman wife. In a sense, then, there is no way back for her even though the men in her life affirm that she is innocent; her suicide is the outcome. For her, not even the punishment of Tarquin could reverse the effects of the crime.

The pathos of Lucrece's fate has not shielded her entirely from criticism. In modern times, she has been faulted both for her compliance with Roman conjugal codes and her suicide, which adds unwarranted self-punishment to the injury she has already suffered. In late antiquity, Saint Augustine had severely criticized Livy's Lucrece in his own work entitled *The City of God*. There he argued that the woman who does not consent in her mind to the rape is innocent – spiritually untainted – and what happens to her body is therefore immaterial. According to Augustine, Lucrece's suicide either betrays guilt or at least makes her guilty of willful self-destruction. The virtuous Christian woman who is raped suffers no spiritual (that is, real) harm unless she inwardly consents; for her to commit suicide would be a mortal sin. (Let us note, however, that the rape of Lucrece was again being used for its leverage, this time by Saint Augustine to dislodge a pagan, Roman world order and institute a new, Christian one.)

The difficulty with Augustine's view is that it produces an almost impossibly watertight division between soul and body, at the same time devaluing the body and the harms it suffers. Lucrece sees her predicament differently:

> Ay me, the bark pilled from the lofty pine,
> His leaves will wither and his sap decay;
> So must my soul, her bark being pilled away.
> (1167-69)

Although Shakespeare's poem is set during early Roman history, before the advent of Christianity, Shakespeare inherits the Christian traditions that include Augustine's teachings. Even while telling the story as a Roman one, Shakespeare is thus aware of subsequent Christian teachings, the language of which he anachronistically incorporates in the poem. He strongly questions those teachings as well as earlier Roman ones.

The problem for the chaste married woman as distinct from the Christian virgin is that she is expected to possess sexual desire but confine it entirely to her husband, even mentally. Husbands, on the other hand, both demanded and distrusted the sexual responsiveness of their wives. This contradiction is fully crystallized in *Othello,* written after *Lucrece* and resembling it in some respects. Desdemona's sexuality unnerves Othello, allowing Iago to implant suspicions. The Desdemona Othello finally appreciates is the sleeping one at whom he gazes lovingly, much as Tarquin gazes at the sleeping Lucrece, before killing her. This Desdemona, however, already resembles a burial sculpture: it would seem that, for the husband, the truly chaste, lovable wife can only be the dead wife.

Lucrece's sexuality is evident in her first, lively encounter with Tarquin, who comes to her house as an honored guest. Their exchange of glances might already have counted for Elizabethans as a form of sexual consciousness and interaction, yet that does not mean Lucrece is guilty. Most social encounters cannot be free of sexual consciousness and of power-gender relations in which both fear and desire are present. Arguably, Tarquin feels as awed by Lucrece in this first encounter as she does by him. It is undeniable that the situation is inherently tempting to Lucrece, yet she gives Tarquin no encouragement, and evidently cannot read the seductively insinuating "text" of his facial expressions and body language. Since she is a hostess, however, and her husband's social representative, she cannot escape this world of public interaction. Insofar as she is compromised even by her social encounter with Tarquin, it will be almost impossible for her to feel inwardly untainted and outwardly unashamed after she has been raped.

For Saint Augustine, the spiritual Christian woman is removed from these social situations, which don't count. She will also be indifferent, as Lucrece is not, to the way things look to others after she has been raped. The Roman men in the poem, anticipating Augustine, declare Lucrece wholly innocent, yet she knows better than they how little this declaration will do for her, or even for her reputation:

> With this they all at once began to say
> Her body's stain her mind untainted clears,
> While with a joyless smile she turns away
> The face, that map which deep impression bears
> Of hard misfortune, carved in it with tears.
>
> (1709-13)

To be a heroine of chastity on her own terms, not setting a bad example to other wives, Lucrece believes she must kill herself, also thereby "healing" herself of the "sickness" of having been raped.

The severity of Lucrece's mental predicament is perhaps most vividly illustrated when she gazes at the Trojan picture, trying to find her new place in the story. She cannot fully identify herself with old Queen Hecuba as tragic victim, and does not want to be identified with the suspect Helen, however powerful and glamorous she may be. The figure on whom she surprisingly yet revealingly fixes is that of Sinon, the traitor who brought about Troy's downfall. She sees Sinon as both a perfect actor and a perfect hypocrite, who defeats all judgments about sincerity, probably including his own. She wants to identify Tarquin with Sinon as the betrayer, yet Sinon also becomes a mocking image confronting her. His deception is so perfect that it represents this poem's equivalent to the vanishing point in *Venus and Adonis;* here, distinctions between guilt and innocence, inner and outer, collapse. Lucrece feels so profoundly undermined in her integrity by this mocking image that she physically attacks the painting. Yet the very violence of her attack – an attack she recognizes as absurd, with the surprising humor she musters on occasion – indicates her inability to clear herself in her own mind or in the eyes of all others. This inability, resulting for her in acute self-consciousness before others, is apparent even when she is facing her own humble servingman:

> But they whose guilt within their bosoms lie
> Imagine every eye beholds their blame;
> For Lucrece thought he blushed to see her shame.
>   (1342-44)

Such is the plight of the innocent woman, as exemplified by Lucrece. Modern readers should have no difficulty understanding it.

The Phoenix and the Turtle

In contrast to the previous poems, *The Phoenix and the Turtle,* published under Shakespeare's full name in a collection called *Love's Martyr* in 1601, concerns true, mutual love. The lovers in the poem are birds, the mythical phoenix and the turtledove. These birds perfectly embody the masculine and feminine attributes and desires of imperfect humans. In this perfect love, the two lovers merge into a single being, thus "confounding" both identity and difference. In keeping with the previous poems, however, the poem is one of mourning for a perfect love that seems to have vanished from the world or perhaps been mythic all along. We cannot be sure whether the birds have simply died or passed beyond an imperfect world when we hear that they "fled / In a mutual flame from hence" (23-24).

This is the Shakespearean poem that has most often been regarded as a "metaphysical" lyric of the kind written by English poets in the seventeenth century, and appreciated in the twentieth century by T. S. Eliot for combining stringent logical argument with passionate feeling. The unusually tight, spare, disciplined language of the poem concurs with its rigorously logical articulation. It would seem that the mutual passion at once celebrated and mourned in Shakespeare's poem cannot even be conceived except in the most logical – but also logic-defying – terms. This perfect love becomes the lost but solemnly recalled ideal for all imperfect human loves.

The scenario of *The Phoenix and the Turtle* is one in which birds are summoned to the funeral of the lovers, which is also to say of love itself. The invitation pointedly excludes all predatory birds of "tyrant wing" (10). Those birds that fit the occasion on account of their mythical properties, like the swan that sings a beautiful song just before it dies or the long-lived crow that reproduces without sexual contact, are called upon to mourn over the ashes of the departed. The passing of the phoenix and the turtle is especially to be mourned since they left "no posterity" (59), meaning no progeny but also no successors like themselves. Their union was one of "married chastity" (61), a condition that seems to imply asexual union rather than the kind of married chastity that creates Lucrece's impossible predicament.

Not only is love lost in this exalted poem, but also, it would seem, the immortality of the phoenix, always reborn from its own ashes. The poem implies that by having become involved even in the most perfect imaginable love, the phoenix has sacrificed its immortality. It has also sacrificed its own singularity in merging with the turtle. Already, then, love has come under the shadow of mortality, even in its most rarefied perfection. When the young man in Shakespeare's sonnets is being persuaded to forego his singleness – that is, to marry and reproduce – he is also being persuaded to accept his own mortality. One of the metaphors for the privileged, solitary condition he is being asked to abandon is that of the phoenix.

Minor and "Dubious" Poems

As regards the minor or "dubious" poems, I will merely note, first, that several poems in *The Passionate Pilgrim* deal saucily with the courtship of Adonis by Venus, and are thus thematically related to Shakespeare's long poem on the subject. Second, if Shakespeare wrote *A Lover's Complaint*, it is his contribution to the contemporary genre of poetic complaint practiced by Samuel Daniel and Edmund Spenser among others. Lucrece's extended "complaint" after she has been raped makes it clear that the poetics of (female) complaint are not alien to Shakespeare. *A Lover's Complaint* consists mainly of a female speaker's complaint of seduction and betrayal by a young man, irresistible to both men and women, who prevails on her by "frankly" confessing his innumerable previous conquests. His most spectacular success has been the seduction of a nun, an unholy triumph now to be redeemed by his true love of her alone. Even though she has been deceived and ruined, she ends up admitting that she would probably be deceived again in exactly the same way. The poem has lent itself to some dubious claims about inherent male and female psychology; although this line of argument seems like a dead end, the poem remains something of a challenge to gendered (and other) reading. Arguments pro and contra Shakespeare's authorship continue, and if nothing else, this strange poem continues to exert pressure on our received ideas about Shakespeare's poetic and stylistic range. The marked differences between the well-attested poems are already hard enough to accommodate in any unified conception of Shakespeare's poetic identity. *A Lover's Complaint* is a marginal poem that still resists any desire on our part to resolve which poems are finally and definitively Shakespearean.

JONATHAN CREWE
Dartmouth College

Note on the Text

THE COPY TEXTS for this edition of the poems are the 1593 First Quarto of *Venus and Adonis*; the 1594 First Quarto of *Lucrece* (in which "The Rape of Lucrece" already appears as a running title); the text of *The Phoenix and the Turtle* in the 1601 first edition of *Love's Martyr* (Folger Library copy); the 1599 second edition (Octavo 2) of *The Passionate Pilgrim* (Huntington Library copy); and *A Lover's Complaint* in the 1609 edition of Shakespeare's sonnets. I have gratefully incorporated much of the editorial work of an earlier Penguin editor, Maurice Evans, and have relied indispensably on textual analysis and collation by previous editors, notably Hyder Rollins, F. T. Prince, and John Roe. The following collation by no means includes all known variants or emendations; it lists only those that are materially significant to the texts printed here.

Venus and Adonis

14 *rein* raine Q1; reigne Q7–10; reine Q11   54 *murders* murthers Q1; smothers Q7+   63 *prey* pray Q1   134 *Ill-nurtured* Il-nurtured Q1; Ill-natured Q9–11   362 *jail* gaile Q1; gaol Q11, 13+   392 *Servilely* Servilly Q1   466 *loss* love Q1   645 *downright* down right Q1   680 *overshoot* over-shut Q1   777 *mermaid's* Marmaids Q1   873 *twine* twined Q1; twine Q7+   888 *court'sy* curt'sie Q1   1095 *sung* song Q1

Lucrece

8 *unhapp'ly* unhap'ly Q1   31 *apology* Appologies Q1   50 *Collatium* Collatium Q1   56 *o'er* ore Q1; o'er Q6+   124 *life's* lives Q1; lifes Q3–4   239 *ay, if* I, if Q1   342 *prey* pray Q1; prey Q6+   425 *Slacked* Slakt Q1; slacked Q2+   506 *falcon* Faulkon Q1   509 *falchion* Fauchion Q1   879 *point'st* poinst Q1; points Q5+   975 *bedrid* bedred Q1   1039 *no-slaughterhouse* no slaughter house Q1; no-slaughter house Q3–4   1310 *tenor* tenure Q1; tenor Q6+   1451 *reign* raigne Q1; raine Q4   1486 *swounds* sounds Q1   1644 *Rome* Roome Q1; Rome Q3+   1713 *in it* it in Q1

The Passionate Pilgrim

1.11 *habit is* habit's in O1; habit is O2–3   **3.11** *Exhale* Exhalst *LLL*; Exhalt O1; Exhale O2–3   **4.10** *her* his O1; her O2–3   **7.10** *thereof* thereof O3; whereof O2   **7.11** *midst* mids O2; midst O3   **14.3** *care* O2; cares O3 **14.27** *moon* houre O1–3   **16.12** *throne* O1–3; thorn *England's Helicon*   **18.20** *humble* humblel O1–3   **18.22** *a new* anew O1–3   **18.26** *calm ere* calme yer O1–3   **18.45** *be* by O1–3   **18.51** *on th'ear* on th'are O1–2; on th'ere O3

A Lover's Complaint

80 *Of one* O one Q   **118** *Came* Can Q   **182** *woo* wovv Q

The Narrative Poems

Venus and Adonis

TO THE
**RIGHT HONORABLE
HENRY WRIOTHESLEY,**
EARL OF SOUTHAMPTON AND BARON OF TITCHFIELD

RIGHT HONORABLE,

    I know not how I shall offend in dedicating my unpolished lines to your lordship, nor how the world will censure me for choosing so strong a prop to support so weak a burden: only, if your honor seem but pleased, I account myself highly praised, and vow to take advantage of all idle hours, till I have honored you with some graver labor. But if the first heir of my invention prove deformed, I shall be sorry it had so noble a godfather, and never after 9 ear so barren a land, for fear it yield me still so bad a har-10 vest. I leave it to your honorable survey, and your honor to your heart's content; which I wish may always answer your own wish, and the world's hopeful expectation.

Your honor's in all duty,
William Shakespeare

*

Dedication: The Earl of Southampton, aged nineteen at the time of this dedication, was a noted literary patron, not averse to "libertine" (sexually licentious) writings **9** *ear* plow, cultivate *Epigraph:* Ovid, *Amores*, I.xv.35–36. "Let what is cheap excite the wonder of the crowd; to me, may golden Apollo minister full cups from the Castalian fount."

Venus and Adonis

Vilia miretur vulgus: mihi flavus Apollo
Pocula Castalia plena ministret aqua.

Even as the sun with purple-colored face 1
Had ta'en his last leave of the weeping morn, 2
Rose-cheeked Adonis hied him to the chase; 3
Hunting he loved, but love he laughed to scorn.
    Sick-thoughted Venus makes amain unto him, 5
    And like a bold-faced suitor 'gins to woo him.

"Thrice fairer than myself," thus she began,
"The field's chief flower, sweet above compare,
Stain to all nymphs, more lovely than a man, 9
More white and red than doves or roses are; 10
    Nature that made thee with herself at strife 11
    Saith that the world hath ending with thy life.

"Vouchsafe, thou wonder, to alight thy steed, 13
And rein his proud head to the saddle bow; 14
If thou wilt deign this favor, for thy meed 15
A thousand honey secrets shalt thou know.
    Here come and sit, where never serpent hisses,
    And being set, I'll smother thee with kisses; 18

---

1 *purple-colored* bright crimson 2 *weeping* i.e., dewy 3 *hied him* hastened
5 *Sick-thoughted* lovesick; *makes amain* speeds 9 *Stain to* blot upon 11 *at strife* struggling to outdo herself 13 *alight* dismount from 14 *saddle bow* curved front of the saddle 15 *deign* condescend to do; *meed* reward 18 *set* seated

19 "And yet not cloy thy lips with loathed satiety,
20 But rather famish them amid their plenty,
   Making them red and pale with fresh variety;
   Ten kisses short as one, one long as twenty.
       A summer's day will seem an hour but short,
       Being wasted in such time-beguiling sport."

   With this she seizeth on his sweating palm,
26 The precedent of pith and livelihood,
27 And trembling in her passion calls it balm,
28 Earth's sovereign salve to do a goddess good.
29   Being so enraged, desire doth lend her force
30   Courageously to pluck him from his horse.

31 Over one arm the lusty courser's rein,
   Under her other was the tender boy,
   Who blushed and pouted in a dull disdain,
34 With leaden appetite, unapt to toy;
       She red and hot as coals of glowing fire,
       He red for shame, but frosty in desire.

37 The studded bridle on a ragged bough
   Nimbly she fastens (O, how quick is love!);
39 The steed is stallèd up, and even now
40 To tie the rider she begins to prove.
41   Backward she pushed him, as she would be thrust,
42   And governed him in strength, though not in lust.

43 So soon was she along as he was down,
   Each leaning on their elbows and their hips;
   Now doth she stroke his cheek, now doth he frown,

---

19 *satiety* excess   **26** *precedent* advance sign; *pith and livelihood* (sexual) vital-
ity and energy   **27** *balm* ointment   **28** *salve* remedy   **29** *enraged* aroused
30 *Courageously* with lusty boldness   **31** *courser* steed   **34** *toy* engage in sex-
ual play   **37** *ragged* rugged   **39** *stallèd up* penned up   **40** *prove* attempt   **41**
would be wished to be   **42** *lust* desire   **43** *along* alongside

And 'gins to chide, but soon she stops his lips,
    And kissing speaks, with lustful language broken,   47
    "If thou wilt chide, thy lips shall never open."

He burns with bashful shame; she with her tears
Doth quench the maiden burning of his cheeks;   50
Then with her windy sighs and golden hairs
To fan and blow them dry again she seeks.
    He saith she is immodest, blames her miss;   53
    What follows more she murders with a kiss.

Even as an empty eagle, sharp by fast,   55
Tires with her beak on feathers, flesh and bone,
Shaking her wings, devouring all in haste,
Till either gorge be stuffed or prey be gone;   58
    Even so she kissed his brow, his cheek, his chin,
    And where she ends she doth anew begin.   60

Forced to content, but never to obey,   61
Panting he lies and breatheth in her face;
She feedeth on the steam as on a prey,   63
And calls it heavenly moisture, air of grace,   64
    Wishing her cheeks were gardens full of flowers,
    So they were dewed with such distilling showers.   66

Look how a bird lies tangled in a net,
So fastened in her arms Adonis lies;
Pure shame and awed resistance made him fret,   69
Which bred more beauty in his angry eyes.   70
    Rain added to a river that is rank   71
    Perforce will force it overflow the bank.

---

47 *broken* interrupted   50 *maiden* virginal   53 *miss* misbehavior   55 *sharp by fast* ravenous for lack of food   58 *gorge* crop   61 *content* acquiesce   63 *steam* hot breath   64 *of grace* given by divine grace   66 *distilling showers* i.e., condensing droplets   69 *awed resistance* subjugated resistance   71 *rank* swollen

Still she entreats, and prettily entreats,
For to a pretty ear she tunes her tale:
75 Still is he sullen, still he lours and frets,
'Twixt crimson shame and anger ashy-pale.
 Being red, she loves him best, and being white,
 Her best is bettered with a more delight.

79 Look how he can, she cannot choose but love,
80 And by her fair immortal hand she swears
81 From his soft bosom never to remove
82 Till he take truce with her contending tears
 Which long have rained, making her cheeks all wet;
 And one sweet kiss shall pay this countless debt.

Upon this promise did he raise his chin,
86 Like a dive-dapper peering through a wave,
Who, being looked on, ducks as quickly in;
So offers he to give what she did crave;
89 But when her lips were ready for his pay,
90 He winks, and turns his lips another way.

91 Never did passenger in summer's heat
More thirst for drink than she for this good turn.
Her help she sees, but help she cannot get;
She bathes in water, yet her fire must burn.
 "O, pity," 'gan she cry, "flint-hearted boy,
 'Tis but a kiss I beg; why art thou coy?

"I have been wooed, as I entreat thee now,
98 Even by the stern and direful god of war,
Whose sinewy neck in battle ne'er did bow,

---

75 *lours* frowns 79 *Look how he can* however he looks 81 *remove* depart
82 *take truce* make peace; *contending* assailing 86 *dive-dapper* dabchick 89
pay payment 91 *passenger* foot traveler 98 *god of war* Mars, god of war and
lover of Venus in Roman mythology

Who conquers where he comes in every jar;   100
  Yet hath he been my captive and my slave,
  And begged for that which thou unasked shalt have.   102

"Over my altars hath he hung his lance,
His battered shield, his uncontrollèd crest,   104
And for my sake hath learned to sport and dance,
To toy, to wanton, dally, smile and jest,   106
  Scorning his churlish drum and ensign red,   107
  Making my arms his field, his tent my bed.   108

"Thus he that overruled I overswayed,   109
Leading him prisoner in a red-rose chain;   110
Strong-tempered steel his stronger strength obeyed,
Yet was he servile to my coy disdain.   112
  O, be not proud, nor brag not of thy might,
  For mastering her that foiled the god of fight!

"Touch but my lips with those fair lips of thine –
Though mine be not so fair, yet are they red –
The kiss shall be thine own as well as mine.
What see'st thou in the ground? Hold up thy head,
  Look in mine eyeballs, there thy beauty lies;   119
  Then why not lips on lips, since eyes in eyes?   120

"Art thou ashamed to kiss? Then wink again,
And I will wink; so shall the day seem night.
Love keeps his revels where there are but twain;
Be bold to play, our sport is not in sight.   124
  These blue-veined violets whereon we lean
  Never can blab, nor know not what we mean.

---

100 *jar* conflict   102 *unasked* without asking   104 *uncontrollèd crest* hel-
met, never bowed in defeat   106 *toy* play; *dally* engage in amorous play
107 *churlish* harsh, unmelodious; *ensign* banner   108 *field* i.e., amorous bat-
tlefield   109 *overswayed* overbore   112 *coy disdain* seductive aloofness   119
lies i.e., is reflected   124 *in sight* in public view, being watched

127 "The tender spring upon thy tempting lip
Shews thee unripe; yet mayst thou well be tasted:
Make use of time, let not advantage slip;
130 Beauty within itself should not be wasted.
        Fair flowers that are not gathered in their prime
        Rot, and consume themselves in little time.

133 "Were I hard-favored, foul, or wrinkled-old,
134 Ill-nurtured, crooked, churlish, harsh in voice,
135 O'erworn, despisèd, rheumatic and cold,
136 Thick-sighted, barren, lean, and lacking juice,
        Then mightst thou pause, for then I were not for thee;
        But having no defects, why dost abhor me?

"Thou canst not see one wrinkle in my brow;
140 Mine eyes are gray and bright and quick in turning;
141 My beauty as the spring doth yearly grow,
142 My flesh is soft and plump, my marrow burning;
        My smooth moist hand, were it with thy hand felt,
        Would in thy palm dissolve, or seem to melt.

"Bid me discourse, I will enchant thine ear,
146 Or like a fairy trip upon the green,
Or like a nymph with long disheveled hair,
Dance on the sands, and yet no footing seen.
149   Love is a spirit all compact of fire,
150   Not gross to sink, but light, and will aspire.

"Witness this primrose bank whereon I lie;
152 These forceless flowers like sturdy trees support me;
153 Two strengthless doves will draw me through the sky

---

127 *tender spring* i.e., boyish down   133 *hard-favored* hard-featured; *foul*
ugly   134 *Ill-nurtured* ill-bred; *crooked* deformed; *churlish* uncouth   135
O'erworn worn out   136 *Thick-sighted* dim-sighted   140 *gray* blue   141
yearly grow annually renews itself   142 *marrow* inner being   146 *trip* dance
149 *compact* composed of   150 *aspire* rise up   152 *forceless* weak   153 *doves*
i.e., the birds by which Venus's chariot is traditionally drawn through the sky

From morn till night, even where I list to sport me.
　Is love so light, sweet boy, and may it be
　That thou should think it heavy unto thee?

"Is thine own heart to thine own face affected?   157
Can thy right hand seize love upon thy left?   158
Then woo thyself, be of thyself rejected,
Steal thine own freedom, and complain on theft.   160
　Narcissus so himself himself forsook,
　And died to kiss his shadow in the brook.   162

"Torches are made to light, jewels to wear,
Dainties to taste, fresh beauty for the use,   164
Herbs for their smell, and sappy plants to bear;   165
Things growing to themselves are growth's abuse.   166
　Seeds spring from seeds and beauty breedeth beauty;
　Thou wast begot; to get it is thy duty.   168

"Upon the earth's increase why shouldst thou feed,   169
Unless the earth with thy increase be fed?   *170*
By law of nature thou art bound to breed,
That thine may live when thou thyself art dead;
　And so in spite of death thou dost survive,
　In that thy likeness still is left alive."

By this the lovesick queen began to sweat,
For where they lay the shadow had forsook them,
And Titan, tirèd in the midday heat,   177
With burning eye did hotly overlook them,   178
　Wishing Adonis had his team to guide,   179
　So he were like him, and by Venus' side.   *180*

---

157 *affected* drawn to (like Narcissus)   158 *Can . . . left* can you possess love
by clasping your own hands   160 *on* of   162 *shadow* image   164 *Dainties*
sweetmeats   165 *sappy* moist and vital   166 *to themselves* for themselves
alone   168 *get* beget   169 *increase* abundance, progeny   177 *Titan* Roman
sun god; *tirèd* attired   178 *overlook* look down on   179 *his team* the horses
that draw his chariot across the sky

181 And now Adonis with a lazy sprite,
    And with a heavy, dark, disliking eye,
183 His louring brows o'erwhelming his fair sight,
    Like misty vapors when they blot the sky,
185   Souring his cheeks, cries "Fie, no more of love!
186   The sun doth burn my face; I must remove."

187 "Ay me," quoth Venus, "young, and so unkind!
188 What bare excuses mak'st thou to be gone!
    I'll sigh celestial breath, whose gentle wind
190 Shall cool the heat of this descending sun;
        I'll make a shadow for thee of my hairs;
        If they burn too, I'll quench them with my tears.

    "The sun that shines from heaven shines but warm,
    And lo I lie between that sun and thee;
    The heat I have from thence doth little harm,
    Thine eye darts forth the fire that burneth me;
        And were I not immortal, life were done
        Between this heavenly and earthly sun.

    "Art thou obdurate, flinty, hard as steel?
200 Nay, more than flint, for stone at rain relenteth.
    Art thou a woman's son, and canst not feel
    What 'tis to love, how want of love tormenteth?
        O, had thy mother borne so hard a mind,
204   She had not brought forth thee, but died unkind.

205 "What am I that thou shouldst contemn me this?
    Or what great danger dwells upon my suit?
    What were thy lips the worse for one poor kiss?

---

181 *sprite* spirit   183 *louring* scowling   185 *Souring* pursing   186 *remove* leave   187 *unkind* cruel, unnatural   188 *bare* poor, shameless   200 *relenteth* wears away   204 *unkind* cruel, unnatural, but here also specifically childless   205 *contemn* disdain; *this* thus

Speak, fair, but speak fair words, or else be mute.
　　Give me one kiss, I'll give it thee again,
　　And one for interest, if thou wilt have twain.　　　　　　*210*

"Fie, lifeless picture, cold and senseless stone,　　　　　　211
Well painted idol, image dull and dead,　　　　　　　　　212
Statue contenting but the eye alone,
Thing like a man, but of no woman bred!
　　Thou art no man, though of a man's complexion,　　　215
　　For men will kiss even by their own direction."　　　　216

This said, impatience chokes her pleading tongue,
And swelling passion doth provoke a pause;
Red cheeks and fiery eyes blaze forth her wrong;　　　　219
Begin judge in love, she cannot right her cause;　　　　　220
　　And now she weeps, and now she fain would speak,
　　And now her sobs do her intendments break.　　　　　222

Sometime she shakes her head, and then his hand;
Now gazeth she on him, now on the ground;
Sometime her arms infold him like a band;　　　　　　　225
She would, he will not in her arms be bound;　　　　　　226
　　And when from thence he struggles to be gone,
　　She locks her lily fingers one in one.

"Fondling," she saith, "since I have hemmed thee here　　229
Within the circuit of this ivory pale,　　　　　　　　　230
I'll be a park, and thou shalt be my deer;
Feed where thou wilt, on mountain or in dale;
　　Graze on my lips, and if those hills be dry,
　　Stray lower, where the pleasant fountains lie.

---

211 *senseless* insensible　212 *idol* image　215 *complexion* appearance　216
by . . . direction instinctively, untaught　219 *blaze forth* both visibly on fire
and making known by heraldic means　220 *she . . . her cause* she cannot be
judge in her own case　222 *intendments* intended utterances　225 *infold*
pinion　226 *would* wishes to　229 *Fondling* i.e., an endearment ("foolish
darling"); *hemmed* confined　230 *pale* both a deer-park fence and light-
colored like ivory

235 "Within this limit is relief enough,
236 Sweet bottom-grass and high delightful plain,
237 Round rising hillocks, brakes obscure and rough,
　　To shelter thee from tempest and from rain:
　　　　Then be my deer, since I am such a park;
240 　　No dog shall rouse thee, though a thousand bark."

　　At this Adonis smiles as in disdain,
242 That in each cheek appears a pretty dimple;
　　Love made those hollows, if himself were slain,
　　He might be buried in a tomb so simple,
245 　　Foreknowing well, if there he came to lie,
　　　　Why, there love lived, and there he could not die.

　　These lovely caves, these round enchanting pits,
248 Opened their mouths to swallow Venus' liking.
　　Being mad before, how doth she now for wits?
250 Struck dead at first, what needs a second striking?
251 　　Poor queen of love, in thine own law forlorn,
　　　　To love a cheek that smiles at thee in scorn.

　　Now which way shall she turn? What shall she say?
　　Her words are done, her woes the more increasing;
　　The time is spent, her object will away,
　　And from her twining arms doth urge releasing.
257 　　"Pity," she cries, "some favor, some remorse!"
　　　　Away he springs, and hasteth to his horse.

259 But lo, from forth a copse that neighbors by,
260 A breeding jennet, lusty, young and proud,
　　Adonis' trampling courser doth espy,

---

235 *relief* sustenance   236 *bottom-grass* valley grass, here with sexual innu-
endo   237 *brakes* thickets   240 *rouse* in hunting, to flush from cover   242
That so that   245 *if* so that if   248 *liking* admiration   250 *at first* already
251 *in . . . forlorn* either "outside your own law of love" or "miserably at a
loss under your own law"   257 *remorse* mercy   259 *copse* thicket of small
trees   260 *breeding jennet* broodmare of a small Spanish breed

And forth she rushes, snorts and neighs aloud.
   The strong-necked steed, being tied unto a tree,
   Breaketh his rein and to her straight goes he.

Imperiously he leaps, he neighs, he bounds,
And now his woven girths he breaks asunder;   266
The bearing earth with his hard hoof he wounds,   267
Whose hollow womb resounds like heaven's thunder;
   The iron bit he crusheth 'tween his teeth,
   Controlling what he was controllèd with.   270

His ears up-pricked, his braided hanging mane
Upon his compassed crest now stand on end;   272
His nostrils drink the air, and forth again,
As from a furnace, vapors doth he send;
   His eye, which scornfully glisters like fire,
   Shows his hot courage and his high desire.   276

Sometime he trots, as if he told the steps,   277
With gentle majesty and modest pride;
Anon he rears upright, curvets and leaps,   279
As who should say "Lo, thus my strength is tried, 280
   And this I do to captivate the eye
   Of the fair breeder that is standing by."

What recketh he his rider's angry stir,   283
His flattering "Holla" or his "Stand, I say"?
What cares he now for curb or pricking spur,
For rich caparisons or trappings gay?   286
   He sees his love, and nothing else he sees,
   For nothing else with his proud sight agrees. 288

---

266 *girths* saddle straps **267** *bearing* weight-bearing, fecund **270** *Controlling* mastering **272** *compassed crest* arched neck **276** *courage* spirit **277** *told* counted **279** *curvets* prances **280** *who* one who; *tried* tested **283** *What recketh he* what does he care for; *stir* agitation **286** *caparisons* trappings **288** *agrees* is agreeable to

Look when a painter would surpass the life
290 In limning out a well-proportioned steed,
His art with nature's workmanship at strife,
As if the dead the living should exceed;
    So did this horse excel a common one
294   In shape, in courage, color, pace and bone.

295 Round-hoofed, short-jointed, fetlocks shag and long,
Broad breast, full eye, small head and nostril wide,
297 High crest, short ears, straight legs and passing strong,
Thin mane, thick tail, broad buttock, tender hide;
    Look what a horse should have he did not lack,
300   Save a proud rider on so proud a back.

301 Sometime he scuds far off, and there he stares;
Anon he starts at stirring of a feather;
303 To bid the wind a base he now prepares,
And where he run or fly they know not whether;
    For through his mane and tail the high wind sings,
    Fanning the hairs, who wave like feathered wings.

He looks upon his love and neighs unto her;
She answers him as if she knew his mind;
Being proud, as females are, to see him woo her,
310 She puts on outward strangeness, seems unkind,
    Spurns at his love and scorns the heat he feels,
    Beating his kind embracements with her heels.

313 Then, like a melancholy malcontent,
314 He vails his tail, that, like a falling plume
Cool shadow to his melting buttock lent;

---

290 *limning out* portraying   294 *courage* spirit   295 *fetlock* part of a horse's
foot; *shag* shaggy   297 *passing* exceptionally   301 *scuds* races; *stares* stands
303 *bid . . . a base* challenge the wind to a race   310 *strangeness* aloofness;
unkind hostile, unnaturally reluctant   313 *melancholy malcontent* complain-
ing, disgruntled courtier, a stock character on the Elizabethan and Jacobean
stage   314 *vails* lowers

He stamps, and bites the poor flies in his fume.   316
   His love, perceiving how he was enraged,
   Grew kinder, and his fury was assuaged.

His testy master goeth about to take him,   319
When, lo, the unbacked breeder, full of fear,   320
Jealous of catching, swiftly doth forsake him,   321
With her the horse, and left Adonis there.
   As they were mad, unto the wood they hie them,   323
   Outstripping crows that strive to over-fly them.

All swoln with chafing, down Adonis sits,   325
Banning his boisterous and unruly beast;   326
And now the happy season once more fits
That lovesick love by pleading may be blest;
   For lovers say the heart hath treble wrong
   When it is barred the aidance of the tongue.   330

An oven that is stopped, or river stayed,
Burneth more hotly, swelleth with more rage;
So of concealèd sorrow may be said,   333
Free vent of words love's fire doth assuage;   334
   But when the heart's attorney once is mute,
   The client breaks, as desperate in his suit.   336

He sees her coming, and begins to glow,
Even as a dying coal revives with wind,
And with his bonnet hides his angry brow,   339
Looks on the dull earth with disturbèd mind,   340
   Taking no notice that she is so nigh,
   For all askance he holds her in his eye.   342

---

316 *fume* anger, frustration   319 *goeth about* circles around   320 *unbacked*
unmounted or unbroken   321 *Jealous* wary   323 *As* as if; *hie them* run off
325 *swoln with chafing* choked up with anger   326 *Banning* cursing   330
aidance help   333 *concealèd* confined   334 *Free vent* unobstructed passage;
assuage diminish   336 *breaks* is broken, or bankrupted   339 *bonnet* hat
342 *all . . . his eye* he looks at her covertly

343 O, what a sight it was wistly to view
344 How she came stealing to the wayward boy,
To note the fighting conflict of her hue,
How white and red each other did destroy!
    But now her cheek was pale, and by and by
    It flashed forth fire, as lightning from the sky.

Now was she just before him as he sat,
350 And like a lowly lover down she kneels;
With one fair hand she heaveth up his hat,
Her other tender hand his fair cheek feels;
    His tend'rer cheek receives her soft hand's print
354   As apt as new-fall'n snow takes any dint.

O, what a war of looks was then between them,
356 Her eyes petitioners to his eyes suing!
357 His eyes saw her eyes as they had not seen them;
Her eyes wooed still, his eyes disdained the wooing;
359   And all this dumb play had his acts made plain
360   With tears which choruslike her eyes did rain.

Full gently now she takes him by the hand,
A lily prisoned in a jail of snow,
Or ivory in an alabaster band:
364 So white a friend engirts so white a foe.
    This beauteous combat, willful and unwilling,
366   Showed like two silver doves that sit a-billing.

367 Once more the engine of her thoughts began:
368 "O fairest mover on this mortal round,
369 Would thou wert as I am, and I a man,

---

343 *wistly* attentively 344 *wayward* reluctant 354 *apt* readily; *dint* imprint 356 *petitioners* seekers of favor; *suing* making a plea 357 *as* as if 359–60 *all this . . . rain* this dumb show was interpreted by a choral commentary of tears 364 *engirts* encloses 366 *Showed* appeared 367 *engine of her thoughts* tongue 368 *mover* moving force; *mortal round* the earth (globe) 369 *Would thou wert* if only you were

My heart all whole as thine, thy heart my wound;   370
   For one sweet look thy help I would assure thee,   371
   Though nothing but my body's bane would cure thee."   372

"Give me my hand," saith he, "why dost thou feel it?"
"Give me my heart," saith she, "and thou shalt have it;
O, give it me, lest thy hard heart do steel it,
And being steeled, soft sighs can never grave it;   376
   Then love's deep groans I never shall regard,   377
   Because Adonis' heart hath made mine hard."

"For shame," he cries, "let go, and let me go;
My day's delight is past, my horse is gone,   380
And 'tis your fault I am bereft him so.
I pray you hence, and leave me here alone;   382
   For all my mind, my thought, my busy care,
   Is how to get my palfrey from the mare."   384

Thus she replies: "Thy palfrey, as he should,
Welcomes the warm approach of sweet desire.
Affection is a coal that must be cooled;   387
Else, suffered, it will set the heart on fire.   388
   The sea hath bounds, but deep desire hath none,
   Therefore no marvel though thy horse be gone.   390

"How like a jade he stood tied to the tree,   391
Servilely mastered with a leathern rein;
But when he saw his love, his youth's fair fee,   393
He held such petty bondage in disdain,
   Throwing the base thong from his bending crest,
   Enfranchising his mouth, his back, his breast.   396

---

370 *thy heart my wound* your heart wounded (a wound) as mine is   371 *thy help* your remedy   372 *Though* even if; *bane* harm, destruction   376 *grave* engrave, make an impression   377 *regard* respond to   382 *hence* go away   384 *palfrey* horse   387 *Affection* desire   388 *suffered* allowed to smolder   391 *jade* inferior horse   393 *fee* due reward   396 *Enfranchising* liberating

"Who sees his true-love in her naked bed,
Teaching the sheets a whiter hue than white,
But, when his glutton eye so full hath fed,
His other agents aim at like delight?
    Who is so faint that dares not be so bold
    To touch the fire, the weather being cold?

"Let me excuse thy courser, gentle boy;
And learn of him, I heartily beseech thee,
To take advantage on presented joy;
Though I were dumb, yet his proceedings teach thee.
    O, learn to love; the lesson is but plain,
    And once made perfect, never lost again."

"I know not love," quoth he, "nor will not know it,
Unless it be a boar, and then I chase it.
'Tis much to borrow, and I will not owe it.
My love to love is love but to disgrace it;
    For I have heard it is a life in death,
    That laughs and weeps and all but with a breath.

"Who wears a garment shapeless and unfinished?
Who plucks the bud before one leaf put forth?
If springing things be any jot diminished,
They wither in their prime, prove nothing worth.
    The colt that's backed and burdened being young
    Loseth his pride, and never waxeth strong.

"You hurt my hand with wringing; let us part,
And leave this idle theme, this bootless chat;
Remove your siege from my unyielding heart,

---

400 *agents* senses and organs **401** *faint* cowardly **405** *on* of **408** *made perfect* fully learned **411** *'Tis much to borrow* the loan creates too large an obligation **412** *My love . . . disgrace it* my only desire regarding love is to demean it **417** *springing* growing **419** *backed* broken in **420** *waxeth* grows **422** *bootless* unprofitable

To love's alarms it will not ope the gate.   424
   Dismiss your vows, your feignèd tears, your flatt'ry;   425
   For where a heart is hard they make no batt'ry."   426

"What, canst thou talk?" quoth she, "hast thou a tongue?
O would thou hadst not, or I had no hearing!
Thy mermaid's voice hath done me double wrong;   429
I had my load before, now pressed with bearing: 430
   Melodious discord, heavenly tune harsh sounding,
   Ears' deep sweet music, and heart's deep sore wounding.

"Had I no eyes but ears, my ears would love
That inward beauty and invisible;
Or were I deaf, thy outward parts would move
Each part in me that were but sensible.   436
   Though neither eyes nor ears, to hear nor see,   437
   Yet should I be in love by touching thee.

"Say that the sense of feeling were bereft me,
And that I could not see, nor hear, nor touch,   440
And nothing but the very smell were left me,
Yet would my love to thee be still as much;
   For from the stillitory of thy face excelling   443
   Comes breath perfumed, that breedeth love by smelling.

"But O, what banquet wert thou to the taste,
Being nurse and feeder of the other four!   446
Would they not wish the feast might ever last,
And bid suspicion double-lock the door,
   Lest jealousy, that sour unwelcome guest,
   Should by his stealing in disturb the feast?"   450

---

424 *alarms* assaults 425 *Dismiss* i.e., disband, like an army 426 *batt'ry* artillery barrage and/or breach in the fortifications 429 *mermaid's voice* i.e., deceivingly seductive 430 *pressed* weighed down 436 *sensible* capable of sensation 437 *Though* though having 443 *stillitory* apparatus for distilling perfumes 446 *four* i.e., four senses

451 Once more the ruby-colored portal opened,
    Which to his speech did honey passage yield;
    Like a red morn, that ever yet betokened
    Wrack to the seaman, tempest to the field,
        Sorrow to shepherds, woe unto the birds,
456   Gusts and foul flaws to herdmen and to herds.

457 This ill presage advisedly she marketh:
    Even as the wind is hushed before it raineth,
    Or as the wolf doth grin before he barketh,
460 Or as the berry breaks before it staineth,
        Or like the deadly bullet of a gun,
        His meaning struck her ere his words begun.

    And at his look she flatly falleth down,
    For looks kill love, and love by looks reviveth;
465 A smile recures the wounding of a frown.
    But blessèd bankrupt that by loss so thriveth!
467   The silly boy, believing she is dead,
        Claps her pale cheek, till clapping makes it red;

    And all amazed brake off his late intent,
470 For sharply he did think to reprehend her,
471 Which cunning love did wittily prevent.
472 Fair fall the wit that can so well defend her!
        For on the grass she lies as she were slain,
        Till his breath breatheth life in her again.

475 He wrings her nose, he strikes her on the cheeks,
    He bends her fingers, holds her pulses hard,
477 He chafes her lips, a thousand ways he seeks

---

451 *portal* gate (Adonis's mouth) 456 *flaws* squalls 457 *presage* omen
465 *recures* heals 467 *silly* simple 470 *reprehend* scold 471 *wittily* clev-
erly 472 *Fair fall* good luck to 475 *wrings* tweaks 477 *chafes* rubs

To mend the hurt that his unkindness marred;   478
  He kisses her, and she, by her good will,   479
  Will never rise, so he will kiss her still.   480

The night of sorrow now is turned to day:
Her two blue windows faintly she upheaveth,   482
Like the fair sun, when in his fresh array
He cheers the morn, and all the earth relieveth;
  And as the bright sun glorifies the sky,
  So is her face illumined with her eye;   486

Whose beams upon his hairless face are fixèd,
As if from thence they borrowed all their shine.
Were never four such lamps together mixèd,   489
Had not his clouded with his brow's repine;   490
  But hers, which through the crystal tears gave light,
  Shone like the moon in water seen by night.

"O, where am I?" quoth she, "in earth or heaven,
Or in the ocean drenched, or in the fire?
What hour is this? Or morn or weary even?   495
Do I delight to die, or life desire?
  But now I lived, and life was death's annoy;   497
  But now I died, and death was lively joy.

"O thou didst kill me, kill me once again.
Thy eyes' shrewd tutor, that hard heart of thine,   500
Hath taught them scornful tricks, and such disdain
That they have murdered this poor heart of mine;
  And these mine eyes, true leaders to their queen,   503
  But for thy piteous lips no more had seen.   504

---

478 *marred* i.e., had done   479 *by her good will* willingly   480 *so* as long as
482 *upheaveth* lifts   486 *illumined* lit up   489 *four . . . lamps* their four eyes
490 *repine* vexation   495 *Or . . . or* either . . . or; *even* evening   497 *But*
even; *annoy* misery   500 *shrewd* cruel, punitive   503 *true . . . queen* trust-
worthy messengers or guides to Venus's heart   504 *piteous* pitying

505 "Long may they kiss each other, for this cure!
506 O, never let their crimson liveries wear!
507 And as they last, their verdure still endure
508 To drive infection from the dangerous year,
509   That the stargazers, having writ on death,
510   May say, the plague is banished by thy breath.

"Pure lips, sweet seals in my soft lips imprinted,
512 What bargains may I make, still to be sealing?
To sell myself I can be well contented,
514 So thou wilt buy, and pay, and use good dealing;
515   Which purchase if thou make, for fear of slips
516   Set thy seal manual on my wax-red lips.

"A thousand kisses buys my heart from me;
And pay them at thy leisure, one by one.
519 What is ten hundred touches unto thee?
520 Are they not quickly told and quickly gone?
      Say for nonpayment that the debt should double,
      Is twenty hundred kisses such a trouble?"

523 "Fair queen," quoth he, "if any love you owe me,
524 Measure my strangeness with my unripe years;
525 Before I know myself, seek not to know me;
526 No fisher but the ungrown fry forbears:
      The mellow plum doth fall, the green sticks fast,
      Or being early plucked is sour to taste.

---

505 *they* i.e., Adonis's lips 506 *crimson liveries wear* i.e., wear out their fresh color (literally, their red servant uniforms) 507 *verdure* freshness 508 *drive . . . year* purge infection like herbs during a plague year 509 *stargazers* astrologers; *writ on death* prophesied an epidemic 512 *still to be* to continue 514 *use good dealing* deal fairly 515 *slips* counterfeit coins 516 *seal manual* signature 519 *touches* kisses, authenticating marks on coins 520 *told* counted 523 *owe* feel for 524 *Measure my strangeness* equate my aloofness 525 *know* i.e., implying sexual knowledge 526 *ungrown fry* small, immature fish

"Look, the world's comforter, with weary gait,   529
His day's hot task hath ended in the west;   *530*
The owl, night's herald, shrieks 'tis very late;
The sheep are gone to fold, birds to their nest;
    And coal-black clouds that shadow heaven's light
    Do summon us to part, and bid good night.

"Now let me say good night and so say you;
If you will say so, you shall have a kiss."
"Good night," quoth she, and, ere he says adieu,
The honey fee of parting tendered is: 538
    Her arms do lend his neck a sweet embrace;
    Incorporate then they seem, face grows to face.   540

Till breathless he disjoined, and backward drew
The heavenly moisture, that sweet coral mouth,
Whose precious taste her thirsty lips well knew,
Whereon they surfeit, yet complain on drouth.   544
    He with her plenty pressed, she faint with dearth,   545
    Their lips together glued, fall to the earth.

Now quick desire hath caught the yielding prey,   547
And gluttonlike she feeds, yet never filleth;
Her lips are conquerors, his lips obey,
Paying what ransom the insulter willeth,   550
    Whose vulture thought doth pitch the price so high   551
    That she will draw his lips' rich treasure dry.

And having felt the sweetness of the spoil,   553
With blindfold fury she begins to forage;
Her face doth reek and smoke, her blood doth boil,   555

---

529 *world's comforter* the sun   **538** *tendered* offered   **540** *Incorporate* merged into one body   **544** *drouth* thirst   **545** *pressed* burdened; *dearth* lack   **547** *quick* lively, swift   **550** *insulter* aggressor   **551** *vulture* greedy   **553** *spoil* plunder   **555** *reek* emit hot vapor

And careless lust stirs up a desperate courage,
557　　Planting oblivion, beating reason back,
558　　Forgetting shame's pure blush and honor's wrack.

Hot, faint and weary, with her hard embracing,
560　Like a wild bird being tamed with too much handling,
561　Or as the fleet-foot roe that's tired with chasing,
562　Or like the froward infant stilled with dandling,
　　　He now obeys and now no more resisteth,
564　　While she takes all she can, not all she listeth.

565　What wax so frozen but dissolves with temp'ring,
　　　And yields at last to every light impression?
567　Things out of hope are compassed oft with vent'ring,
568　Chiefly in love, whose leave exceeds commission:
569　　Affection faints not like a pale-faced coward,
570　　But then woos best when most his choice is froward.

571　When he did frown, O had she then gave over,
　　　Such nectar from his lips she had not sucked.
　　　Foul words and frowns must not repel a lover;
　　　What though the rose have prickles, yet 'tis plucked.
　　　　Were beauty under twenty locks kept fast,
　　　　Yet love breaks through, and picks them all at last.

For pity now she can no more detain him;
The poor fool prays her that he may depart.
She is resolved no longer to restrain him;

---

557 *Planting oblivion* instilling thoughtlessness　558 *wrack* ruin　561 *roe* species of small deer　562 *froward* fretful, disgruntled; *dandling* gentle rocking up and down　564 *listeth* wishes for　565 *temp'ring* softening and molding　567 *out of hope* beyond hope; *compassed* achieved; *vent'ring* venturing 568 *leave exceeds commission* permitted to take liberties beyond what is strictly allowed　569 *Affection* desire　570 *his choice is froward* the one he has chosen is unwilling　571 *gave over* given up

Bids him farewell, and look well to her heart,   580
  The which by Cupid's bow she doth protest
  He carries thence incagèd in his breast.   582

"Sweet boy," she says, "this night I'll waste in sorrow,
For my sick heart commands mine eyes to watch.
Tell me, love's master, shall we meet tomorrow?
Say, shall we, shall we? Wilt thou make the match?"   586
  He tells her, no, tomorrow he intends
  To hunt the boar with certain of his friends.

"The boar!" quoth she, whereat a sudden pale,
Like lawn being spread upon the blushing rose,   590
Usurps her cheek; she trembles at his tale,
And on his neck her yoking arms she throws.
  She sinketh down, still hanging by his neck,
  He on her belly falls, she on her back.

Now is she in the very lists of love,   595
Her champion mounted for the hot encounter.   596
All is imaginary she doth prove;   597
He will not manage her, although he mount her;   598
  That worse than Tantalus' is her annoy,   599
  To clip Elysium and to lack her joy.   600

Even so poor birds, deceived with painted grapes,   601
Do surfeit by the eye and pine the maw;   602
Even so she languisheth in her mishaps

---

580 *look well to* take good care of 582 *incagèd* caged 586 *match* bargain
590 *lawn* fine, semitransparent linen 595 *lists* place set up for knightly
jousting 596 *Her champion . . . encounter* her knight is mounted for "bat-
tle" (he is astride her) 597 *imaginary* only in the imagination; *prove* experi-
ence 598 *manage* ride her skillfully 599 *Tantalus* mythological character
in the underworld, tormented by thirst; *annoy* suffering 600 *clip* embrace;
Elysium paradise in classical mythology 601 *Even so* just as; *painted grapes*
(the Greek painter Zeuxis was said to have painted grapes so realistically that
birds pecked at them) 602 *surfeit* feed to excess; *pine the maw* starve the
stomach

604 As those poor birds that helpless berries saw.
605   The warm effect which she in him finds missing
      She seeks to kindle with continual kissing.

But all in vain, good queen, it will not be,
608 She hath assayed as much as may be proved:
609 Her pleading hath deserved a greater fee;
610 She's Love, she loves, and yet she is not loved.
      "Fie, fie," he says, "you crush me, let me go;
612   You have no reason to withhold me so."

613 "Thou hadst been gone," quoth she, "sweet boy, ere this,
      But that thou toldst me thou wouldst hunt the boar.
      O, be advised: thou knowst not what it is
616 With javelin's point a churlish swine to gore,
617   Whose tushes never sheathed he whetteth still,
618   Like to a mortal butcher bent to kill.

619 "On his bow-back he hath a battle set
620 Of bristly pikes that ever threat his foes;
621 His eyes like glowworms shine when he doth fret;
622 His snout digs sepulchers where'er he goes;
623   Being moved, he strikes whate'er is in his way,
      And whom he strikes his crookèd tushes slay.

"His brawny sides, with hairy bristles armed,
626 Are better proof than thy spear's point can enter;
      His short thick neck cannot be easily harmed;
628 Being ireful, on the lion he will venter:
      The thorny brambles and embracing bushes,
630   As fearful of him, part, through whom he rushes.

---

604 *helpless* affording no help   605 *warm effect* arousal   608 *assayed* tried;
proved attempted   609 *fee* payment   612 *withhold* detain   613 *hadst* would
have   616 *churlish* rough, brutish; *gore* pierce, wound   617 *tushes* tusks;
whetteth sharpens, prepares   618 *mortal* deadly   619 *bow-back* arched back;
battle military array   620 *pikes* sharp infantry weapons   621 *fret* get angry
622 *sepulchers* graves   623 *moved* enraged   626 *better proof* more impene-
trable (literally, harder steel)   628 *ireful* angry; *venter* venture

"Alas, he nought esteems that face of thine,
To which love's eyes pays tributary gazes;
Nor thy soft hands, sweet lips and crystal eyne,   633
Whose full perfection all the world amazes;
    But having thee at vantage – wondrous dread! –   635
    Would root these beauties as he roots the mead.   636

"O, let him keep his loathsome cabin still;   637
Beauty hath nought to do with such foul fiends.
Come not within his danger by thy will;   639
They that thrive well take counsel of their friends.   640
    When thou didst name the boar, not to dissemble,
    I feared thy fortune, and my joints did tremble.

"Didst thou not mark my face? Was it not white?   643
Saw'st thou not signs of fear lurk in mine eye?
Grew I not faint, and fell I not downright?   645
Within my bosom, whereon thou dost lie,
    My boding heart pants, beats, and takes no rest,   647
    But like an earthquake shakes thee on my breast.

"For where love reigns, disturbing jealousy   649
Doth call himself affection's sentinel;   650
Gives false alarms, suggesteth mutiny,   651
And in a peaceful hour doth cry "Kill, kill!"
    Distempering gentle love in his desire,   653
    As air and water do abate the fire.

"This sour informer, this bate-breeding spy,   655
This canker that eats up love's tender spring,   656
This carry-tale, dissentious jealousy,   657

---

633 *eyne* eyes 635 *at vantage* in his power 636 *root* uproot 637 *cabin* den 639 *his danger* power to harm you 643 *mark* take note of 645 *downright* immediately, prostrate 647 *boding* foreboding 649 *jealousy* sexual jealousy but also watchful apprehension 650 *affection* passion 651 *suggesteth* brings to mind 653 *Distempering* upsetting 655 *bate-breeding* troublemaking 656 *canker* plant disease 657 *dissentious* causing dissention

That sometime true news, sometime false doth bring,
   Knocks at my heart, and whispers in mine ear
660   That if I love thee I thy death should fear.

"And more than so, presenteth to mine eye
662 The picture of an angry chafing boar
Under whose sharp fangs on his back doth lie
664 An image like thyself, all stained with gore;
   Whose blood upon the fresh flowers being shed
   Doth make them droop with grief and hang the head.

"What should I do, seeing thee so indeed,
668 That tremble at th' imagination?
The thought of it doth make my faint heart bleed,
670 And fear doth teach it divination:
   I prophesy thy death, my living sorrow,
   If thou encounter with the boar tomorrow.

"But if thou needs wilt hunt, be ruled by me;
674 Uncouple at the timorous flying hare,
Or at the fox which lives by subtlety,
676 Or at the roe which no encounter dare.
677   Pursue these fearful creatures o'er the downs,
678   And on thy well-breathed horse keep with thy hounds.

679 "And when thou hast on foot the purblind hare,
680 Mark the poor wretch, to overshoot his troubles,
How he outruns the wind, and with what care
682 He cranks and crosses with a thousand doubles.
683   The many musits through the which he goes
   Are like a labyrinth to amaze his foes.

---

662 *chafing* raging 664 *gore* blood 668 *imagination* image 670 *divination* prophecy 674 *Uncouple* let the hounds loose 676 *roe* small deer 677 *fearful* timid 678 *well-breathed* sound in wind 679 *purblind* dim-sighted 680 *overshoot* overrun, lose track 682 *cranks* twists; *crosses* crisscrosses; *doubles* doublings-back 683 *musits* escape holes in the vegetation

"Sometime he runs among a flock of sheep,
To make the cunning hounds mistake their smell,
And sometime where earth-delving conies keep,   687
To stop the loud pursuers in their yell;   688
    And sometime sorteth with a herd of deer: 689
    Danger deviseth shifts; wit waits on fear.   690

"For there his smell with others being mingled,
The hot scent-snuffing hounds are driven to doubt,
Ceasing their clamorous cry till they have singled
With much ado the cold fault cleanly out.   694
    Then do they spend their mouths; echo replies,   695
    As if another chase were in the skies.

"By this, poor Wat, far off upon a hill,   697
Stands on his hinder legs with listening ear,
To hearken if his foes pursue him still:
Anon their loud alarums he doth hear;   700
    And now his grief may be comparèd well
    To one sore sick that hears the passing bell.

"Then shalt thou see the dew-bedabbled wretch
Turn, and return, indenting with the way;   704
Each envious brier his weary legs do scratch,
Each shadow makes him stop, each murmur stay;
    For misery is trodden on by many,
    And being low, never relieved by any.

"Lie quietly and hear a little more;
Nay, do not struggle, for thou shalt not rise.   *710*
To make thee hate the hunting of the boar,

---

687 *conies* rabbits 688 *loud pursuers . . . yell* baying hounds 689 *sorteth*
consorts, blends in 690 *shifts* tricks; *wit . . . fear* i.e., fear makes us clever
694 *cold fault* mingled scents; *cleanly* distinctly 695 *spend their mouths* cry
out 697 *Wat* folk name for a hare 700 *alarums* calls to arms 704 *indent-
ing* zigzagging

712 Unlike myself thou hear'st me moralize,
         Applying this to that, and so to so;
         For love can comment upon every woe.

715 "Where did I leave?" "No matter where," quoth he;
     "Leave me, and then the story aptly ends.
     The night is spent." "Why, what of that?" quoth she.
     "I am," quoth he, "expected of my friends;
         And now 'tis dark, and going I shall fall."
720   "In night," quoth she, "desire sees best of all.

     "But if thou fall, O, then imagine this,
     The earth, in love with thee, thy footing trips,
     And all is but to rob thee of a kiss.
724 Rich preys make true men thieves; so do thy lips
725   Make modest Dian cloudy and forlorn,
726   Lest she should steal a kiss and die forsworn.

     "Now of this dark night I perceive the reason:
728 Cynthia for shame obscures her silver shine,
729 Till forging nature be condemned of treason,
730 For stealing molds from heaven that were divine,
731   Wherein she framed thee, in high heaven's despite,
         To shame the sun by day and her by night.

733 "And therefore hath she bribed the destinies
734 To cross the curious workmanship of nature,
735 To mingle beauty with infirmities

---

712 *moralize* give cautionary advice   715 *leave* leave off   724 *Rich preys . . .
thieves* large prizes make honest men thieves   725 *Dian* moon goddess of
chastity and hunting in Roman mythology; *cloudy and forlorn* somber and
melancholy (literally, clouded over)   726 *forsworn* having broken her vow of
chastity   728 *Cynthia* another name for the moon   729 *forging* creating,
counterfeiting   731 *framed* made; *in despite* in spite of, to spite   733 *she* i.e.,
the moon; *destinies* fates   734 *cross* thwart; *curious* skillful, intricate   735
infirmities ailments

And pure perfection with impure defeature,   736
  Making it subject to the tyranny
  Of mad mischances and much misery;

"As burning fevers, agues pale and faint,   739
Life-poisoning pestilence and frenzies wood,   740
The marrow-eating sickness whose attaint   741
Disorder breeds by heating of the blood,
  Surfeits, imposthumes, grief and damned despair,   743
  Swear nature's death for framing thee so fair.   744

"And not the least of all these maladies   745
But in one minute's fight brings beauty under:
Both favor, savor, hue and qualities,   747
Whereat th' impartial gazer late did wonder,   748
  Are on the sudden wasted, thawed and done,   749
  As mountain snow melts with the midday sun.   750

"Therefore, despite of fruitless chastity,
Love-lacking vestals and self-loving nuns,   752
That on the earth would breed a scarcity
And barren dearth of daughters and of sons,
  Be prodigal: the lamp that burns by night   755
  Dries up his oil to lend the world his light.

"What is thy body but a swallowing grave,
Seeming to bury that posterity   758
Which by the rights of time thou needs must have,   759

---

736 *defeature* disfigurement   739 *As* such as; *agues* shivering fits   740 *pestilence* plague; *wood* mad   741 *marrow-eating sickness* probably syphilis; *attaint* infection   743 *Surfeits* diseases of gluttonous excess; *imposthumes* abscesses   744 *Swear nature's death* swear to destroy nature and all her works   745–46 *not the least . . . beauty under* even the slightest of these can overthrow beauty in a minute   747 *favor* appearance; *savor* appealing quality   748 *impartial gazer* unbiased onlooker   749 *wasted* laid waste; *thawed* melted   752 *vestals* Roman virgins sworn to chastity   755 *prodigal* freespending   758 *posterity* progeny   759 *rights of time* i.e., when they fall due

760 If thou destroy them not in dark obscurity?
         If so, the world will hold thee in disdain,
762   Sith in thy pride so fair a hope is slain.

     "So in thyself thyself art made away,
764 A mischief worse than civil home-bred strife,
     Or theirs whose desperate hands themselves do slay,
766 Or butcher sire that reaves his son of life.
767   Foul cankering rust the hidden treasure frets,
         But gold that's put to use more gold begets."

     "Nay, then," quoth Adon, "you will fall again
770 Into your idle overhandled theme;
     The kiss I gave you is bestowed in vain,
     And all in vain you strive against the stream;
         For by this black-faced night, desire's foul nurse,
774   Your treatise makes me like you worse and worse.

     "If love have lent you twenty thousand tongues,
     And every tongue more moving than your own,
     Bewitching like the wanton mermaid's songs,
778 Yet from mine ear the tempting tune is blown;
779   For know, my heart stands armèd in mine ear,
780   And will not let a false sound enter there;

     "Lest the deceiving harmony should run
782 Into the quiet closure of my breast;
     And then my little heart were quite undone,
784 In his bedchamber to be barred of rest.
         No, lady, no, my heart longs not to groan,
         But soundly sleeps, while now it sleeps alone.

---

762 *Sith* since 764 *mischief* evil, misfortune 766 *sire* father; *reaves* robs
767 *cankering* corroding; *frets* corrodes 770 *idle* futile; *overhandled* hackneyed 774 *treatise* argument 778 *blown* blown away 779 *armèd* on guard 782 *closure* enclosure 784 *barred of* denied

"What have you urged that I cannot reprove?   787
The path is smooth that leadeth on to danger;
I hate not love, but your device in love   789
That lends embracements unto every stranger.   790
    You do it for increase: O strange excuse,   791
    When reason is the bawd to lust's abuse!   792

"Call it not love, for love to heaven is fled
Since sweating lust on earth usurped his name;
Under whose simple semblance he hath fed   795
Upon fresh beauty, blotting it with blame;
    Which the hot tyrant stains and soon bereaves,   797
    As caterpillars do the tender leaves.

"Love comforteth like sunshine after rain,
But lust's effect is tempest after sun;   800
Love's gentle spring doth always fresh remain,
Lust's winter comes ere summer half be done;
    Love surfeits not, lust like a glutton dies;   803
    Love is all truth, lust full of forgèd lies.

"More I could tell, but more I dare not say;
The text is old, the orator too green.   806
Therefore, in sadness, now I will away;   807
My face is full of shame, my heart of teen: 808
    Mine ears that to your wanton talk attended
    Do burn themselves for having so offended."   810

With this he breaketh from the sweet embrace
Of those fair arms which bound him to her breast,
And homeward through the dark laund runs apace;   813

---

787 *urged* advocated 789 *device* practice 791 *increase* propagation 792
bawd . . . abuse pimp who facilitates lust's abuses 795 *simple semblance* in-
nocent appearance 797 *the hot tyrant* i.e., lust; *bereaves* robs, lays waste
803 *surfeits* feeds to excess 806 *green* inexperienced 807 *in sadness* seri-
ously 808 *teen* vexation 813 *laund* glade

Leaves love upon her back deeply distressed.
  Look how a bright star shooteth from the sky,
  So glides he in the night from Venus' eye;

Which after him she darts, as one on shore
Gazing upon a late-embarkèd friend,
Till the wild waves will have him seen no more,
820 Whose ridges with the meeting clouds contend;
  So did the merciless and pitchy night
822   Fold in the object that did feed her sight.

Whereat amazed as one that unaware
Hath dropped a precious jewel in the flood,
825 Or 'stonished as night wanderers often are,
826 Their light blown out in some mistrustful wood;
  Even so confounded in the dark she lay
828   Having lost the fair discovery of her way.

And now she beats her heart, whereat it groans,
830 That all the neighbor caves, as seeming troubled,
831 Make verbal repetition of her moans;
832 Passion on passion deeply is redoubled:
  "Ay me!" she cries, and twenty times, "Woe, woe!"
  And twenty echoes twenty times cry so.

835 She, marking them, begins a wailing note,
And sings extemporally a woeful ditty;
837 How love makes young men thrall, and old men dote;
838 How love is wise in folly, foolish witty:
839   Her heavy anthem still concludes in woe,
840   And still the choir of echoes answer so.

---

822 *Fold in* enfold 825 *'stonished* startled, dismayed 826 *mistrustful* unnerving 828 *discovery* i.e., source of illumination 830 *neighbor* neighboring 831 *Make . . . moans* i.e., echo her laments (recalling the classical myth of Echo and Narcissus) 832 *Passion* lamentation 835 *marking* noticing, paying attention to 837 *thrall* captive; *dote* become foolishly obsessed 838 *wise . . . witty* love's wisdom is folly, its cleverness foolish 839 *anthem* choral song, poem

Her song was tedious, and outwore the night,   841
For lovers' hours are long, though seeming short:
If pleased themselves, others, they think, delight
In suchlike circumstance, with suchlike sport.   844
    Their copious stories, oftentimes begun,   845
    End without audience, and are never done.

For who hath she to spend the night withal
But idle sounds resembling parasites,   848
Like shrill-tongued tapsters answering every call,   849
Soothing the humor of fantastic wits?   850
    She says "'Tis so"; they answer all "'Tis so,"
    And would say after her if she said "No."

Lo, here the gentle lark, weary of rest,
From his moist cabinet mounts up on high,   854
And wakes the morning, from whose silver breast
The sun ariseth in his majesty;
    Who doth the world so gloriously behold
    That cedar tops and hills seem burnished gold.

Venus salutes him with this fair good morrow:
"O thou clear god, and patron of all light,   860
From whom each lamp and shining star doth borrow
The beauteous influence that makes him bright,
    There lives a son that sucked an earthly mother   863
    May lend thee light, as thou dost lend to other."

This said, she hasteth to a myrtle grove,   865
Musing the morning is so much o'erworn,   866

---

841 *outwore* outlasted, wore out   844 *circumstance* elaborate detail   845 *oftentimes begun* i.e., much repeated   848 *parasites* fawning dependents (who echo a patron)   849 *tapsters . . . call* taproom boys responding to every patron's call   850 *humor* whim; *fantastic wits* minds made capricious by drink   854 *moist cabinet* dewy nest   860 *clear* bright   863 *a son . . . mother* (in the classical myth, related by Ovid, Adonis was not, in fact, nursed by an "earthly mother")   865 *myrtle* tree associated with Venus   866 *Musing* wondering at (Adonis's failure to appear)

And yet she hears no tidings of her love;
She hearkens for his hounds and for his horn.
869 Anon she hears them chant it lustily,
870 And all in haste she coasteth to the cry.

And as she runs, the bushes in the way
Some catch her by the neck, some kiss her face,
Some twine about her thigh to make her stay;
874 She wildly breaketh from their strict embrace,
875 Like a milch doe, whose swelling dugs do ache,
876 Hasting to feed her fawn hid in some brake.

877 By this she hears the hounds are at a bay,
Whereat she starts, like one that spies an adder
879 Wreathed up in fatal folds just in his way,
880 The fear whereof doth make him shake and shudder:
  Even so the timorous yelping of the hounds
882 Appals her senses and her spirit confounds.

For now she knows it is no gentle chase,
884 But the blunt boar, rough bear, or lion proud,
Because the cry remaineth in one place,
Where fearfully the dogs exclaim aloud.
887 Finding their enemy to be so curst,
888 They all strain court'sy who shall cope him first.

This dismal cry rings sadly in her ear,
890 Through which it enters to surprise her heart,
891 Who, overcome by doubt and bloodless fear,
With cold-pale weakness numbs each feeling part;
  Like soldiers when their captain once doth yield,
  They basely fly and dare not stay the field.

---

869 *Anon* at once; *chant it* give cry 870 *coasteth* moves toward 874 *strict* constricting 875 *milch doe* nursing doe 876 *brake* thicket 877 *at a bay* halted before a dangerous animal at bay 879 *Wreathed* coiled; *fatal* deadly, ominous 882 *confounds* abashes 884 *blunt* rough 887 *curst* fierce 888 *They . . . first* they all hang back politely to let another attack first 890 *surprise* take by surprise 891 *bloodless* pale-faced

Thus stands she in a trembling ecstasy;   895
Till, cheering up her senses all dismayed,
She tells them 'tis a causeless fantasy,
And childish error that they are afraid;
    Bids them leave quaking, bids them fear no more;
    And with that word she spied the hunted boar,   900

Whose frothy mouth, bepainted all with red,
Like milk and blood being mingled both together,
A second fear through all her sinews spread,
Which madly hurries her she knows not whither:
    This way she runs, and now she will no further,
    But back retires to rate the boar for murther.   906

A thousand spleens bear her a thousand ways;   907
She treads the path that she untreads again;
Her more than haste is mated with delays,   909
Like the proceedings of a drunken brain,   910
    Full of respects, yet nought at all respecting,   911
    In hand with all things, nought at all effecting. 912

Here kenneled in a brake she finds a hound,   913
And asks the weary caitiff for his master;   914
And there another licking of his wound,
'Gainst venomed sores the only sovereign plaster;   916
    And here she meets another sadly scowling,
    To whom she speaks, and he replies with howling.

When he hath ceased his ill-resounding noise,
Another flap-mouthed mourner, black and grim,   920
Against the welkin volleys out his voice;   921

---

895 *in . . . ecstasy* beside herself   906 *rate* berate   907 *spleens* conflicting impulses   909 *mated* halted, coupled with   911 *respects* considerations; *respecting* considering   912 *In hand* busy   913 *brake* thicket   914 *caitiff* wretch   916 *venomed* infected; *plaster* remedy   920 *flap-mouthed* with large, loose lips   921 *welkin* sky

Another and another answer him,
 Clapping their proud tails to the ground below,
 Shaking their scratched ears, bleeding as they go.

Look how the world's poor people are amazed
926 At apparitions, signs and prodigies,
Whereon with fearful eyes they long have gazed,
928 Infusing them with dreadful prophecies;
 So she at these sad signs draws up her breath,
930 And, sighing it again, exclaims on death.

931 "Hard-favored tyrant, ugly, meager, lean,
Hateful divorce of love" – thus chides she death –
933 "Grim-grinning ghost, earth's worm, what dost thou mean
To stifle beauty and to steal his breath
 Who when he lived, his breath and beauty set
936 Gloss on the rose, smell to the violet?

"If he be dead – O no, it cannot be,
Seeing his beauty, thou shouldst strike at it –
O yes, it may; thou hast no eyes to see,
940 But hatefully at random dost thou hit:
941 Thy mark is feeble age, but thy false dart
 Mistakes that aim and cleaves an infant's heart.

943 "Hadst thou but bid beware, then he had spoke,
And, hearing him, thy power had lost his power.
945 The destinies will curse thee for this stroke;
They bid thee crop a weed, thou pluckst a flower.
 Love's golden arrow at him should have fled,
948 And not death's ebon dart, to strike him dead.

---

926 *prodigies* unnatural phenomena 928 *Infusing . . . prophecies* reading them as omens 930 *exclaims on* rails against 931 *Hard-favored* grim-featured 933 *earth's worm* lowest of the creatures (?), consumer of all life (?) 936 *Gloss* sheen 941 *mark* proper target 943 *bid beware* give warning 945 *destinies* fates 948 *ebon* black, like ebony

"Dost thou drink tears, that thou provok'st such weeping?
What may a heavy groan advantage thee?   950
Why hast thou cast into eternal sleeping
Those eyes that taught all other eyes to see?
   Now nature cares not for thy mortal vigor,   953
   Since her best work is ruined with thy rigor."   954

Here overcome as one full of despair,
She vailed her eyelids, who, like sluices, stopped   956
The crystal tide that from her two cheeks fair
In the sweet channel of her bosom dropped;
   But through the floodgates breaks the silver rain,   959
   And with his strong course opens them again.   960

O, how her eyes and tears did lend and borrow!   961
Her eye seen in the tears, tears in her eye;
Both crystals, where they viewed each other's sorrow,   963
Sorrow that friendly sighs sought still to dry;
   But like a stormy day, now wind, now rain,
   Sighs dry her cheeks, tears make them wet again.

Variable passions throng her constant woe,   967
As striving who should best become her grief;   968
All entertained, each passion labors so   969
That every present sorrow seemeth chief,   970
   But none is best; then join they all together,
   Like many clouds consulting for foul weather.   972

By this, far off she hears some huntsman halloo;
A nurse's song ne'er pleased her babe so well.
The dire imagination she did follow   975

---

953 *mortal vigor* death-dealing power   954 *rigor* pitilessness   956 *vailed* lowered; *sluices* floodgates   959 *silver rain* tears   961 *lend and borrow* reflect each other   963 *crystals* mirrors   967 *Variable* rapidly fluctuating   968 *become* be fitted to   969 *entertained* given admission   970 *every . . . sorrow* each successive sorrow   972 *consulting* combining   975 *dire imagination* deadly image (of Adonis's death); *follow* accede to

This sound of hope doth labor to expel;
   For now reviving joy bids her rejoice,
   And flatters her it is Adonis' voice.

Whereat her tears began to turn their tide,
980 Being prisoned in her eye like pearls in glass;
981 Yet sometimes falls an orient drop beside,
   Which her cheek melts, as scorning it should pass
      To wash the foul face of the sluttish ground,
      Who is but drunken when she seemeth drowned.

985 O hard-believing love, how strange it seems
986 Not to believe, and yet too credulous!
987 Thy weal and woe are both of them extremes;
   Despair and hope makes thee ridiculous:
      The one doth flatter thee in thoughts unlikely,
990   In likely thoughts the other kills thee quickly.

991 Now she unweaves the web that she hath wrought:
   Adonis lives, and death is not to blame;
993 It was not she that called him all to nought:
   Now she adds honors to his hateful name;
995   She clepes him king of graves, and grave for kings,
996   Imperious supreme of all mortal things.

"No, no," quoth she, "sweet death, I did but jest;
   Yet pardon me, I felt a kind of fear
   When as I met the boar, that bloody beast,
1000 Which knows no pity, but is still severe:
1001   Then, gentle shadow – truth I must confess –
      I railed on thee, fearing my love's decease.

---

981 *orient* clear, flawless   985 *hard-believing* skeptical   986 *credulous* gullible
987 *weal* well-being   991 *web* i.e., of anxious imaginings   993 *called . . .
nought* abused   995 *clepes* calls   996 *Imperious supreme* supreme ruler
1000 *severe* pitiless   1001 *shadow* specter

"'Tis not my fault: the boar provoked my tongue;
Be wreaked on him, invisible commander;   1004
'Tis he, foul creature, that hath done thee wrong;
I did but act, he's author of thy slander.   1006
  Grief hath two tongues, and never woman yet
  Could rule them both without ten women's wit."

Thus, hoping that Adonis is alive,
Her rash suspect she doth extenuate;   1010
And that his beauty may the better thrive,
With death she humbly doth insinuate;   1012
  Tells him of trophies, statues, tombs, and stories   1013
  His victories, his triumphs and his glories.

"O Jove," quoth she, "how much a fool was I   1015
To be of such a weak and silly mind
To wail his death who lives, and must not die
Till mutual overthrow of mortal kind.   1018
  For he being dead, with him is beauty slain,
  And, beauty dead, black chaos comes again.   1020

"Fie, fie, fond love, thou art as full of fear   1021
As one with treasure laden, hemmed with thieves;   1022
Trifles unwitnessèd with eye or ear
Thy coward heart with false bethinking grieves."   1024
  Even at this word she hears a merry horn,
  Whereat she leaps that was but late forlorn.

As falcons to the lure, away she flies;   1027
The grass stoops not, she treads on it so light;

1004 *wreaked* revenged   1006 *author* cause; *thy slander* your being slandered
1010 *suspect* suspicion   1012 *insinuate* flatter to gain favor   1013 *trophies*
monuments; *stories* relates   1015 *Jove* king of the gods in Roman mythology
1018 *mutual* general; *mortal kind* humanity, all living creatures   1020
beauty . . . again the death of ideal beauty, an emanation of the divine, re-
turns creation to primordial chaos   1021 *fond* foolish   1022 *hemmed with*
captured by   1024 *false bethinking* mistaken imagining   1027 *lure* decoy
for training falcons

And in her haste unfortunately spies
1030 The foul boar's conquest on her fair delight;
     Which seen, her eyes, as murdered with the view,
     Like stars ashamed of day, themselves withdrew;

Or as the snail, whose tender horns being hit,
Shrinks backward in his shelly cave with pain,
And there all smothered up in shade doth sit,
Long after fearing to creep forth again;
     So at his bloody view her eyes are fled
     Into the deep-dark cabins of her head;

1039 Where they resign their office and their light
1040 To the disposing of her troubled brain;
1041 Who bids them still consort with ugly night,
     And never wound the heart with looks again;
1043   Who, like a king perplexèd in his throne,
1044   By their suggestion gives a deadly groan:

1045 Whereat each tributary subject quakes,
1046 As when the wind, imprisoned in the ground,
1047 Struggling for passage, earth's foundation shakes,
     Which with cold terror doth men's minds confound.
1049   This mutiny each part doth so surprise,
1050   That from their dark beds once more leap her eyes;

And being opened, threw unwilling light
1052 Upon the wide wound that the boar had trenched
1053 In his soft flank; whose wonted lily-white

1039–40 *Where . . . brain* they yield their independent vision to the control of her disordered mind   1041 *Who* the brain   1043 *perplexèd* anxiously bewildered   1044 *their suggestion* i.e., what they have shown him   1045 *tributary* tribute-paying; *subject* i.e., faculty of the heart   1046–47 *As when . . . shakes* the ancient theory that earthquakes are caused by imprisoned wind, mentioned by Aristotle   1047 *for passage* to escape   1049 *mutiny* uprising; *part* organ   1052 *trenched* cut deeply   1053 *wonted* usual

With purple tears that his wound wept was drenched:
  No flower was nigh, no grass, herb, leaf or weed,
  But stole his blood and seemed with him to bleed.

This solemn sympathy poor Venus noteth:
Over one shoulder doth she hang her head;
Dumbly she passions, frantically she doteth;   1059
She thinks he could not die, he is not dead.   *1060*
  Her voice is stopped, her joints forget to bow;   1061
  Her eyes are mad that they have wept till now.   1062

Upon his hurt she looks so steadfastly   1063
That her sight dazzling makes the wound seem three;   1064
And then she reprehends her mangling eye   1065
That makes more gashes where no breach should be:
  His face seems twain, each several limb is doubled,   1067
  For oft the eye mistakes, the brain being troubled.

"My tongue cannot express my grief for one,
And yet," quoth she, "behold two Adons dead!   *1070*
My sighs are blown away, my salt tears gone,
Mine eyes are turned to fire, my heart to lead;
  Heavy heart's lead, melt at mine eyes' red fire!
  So shall I die by drops of hot desire.

"Alas, poor world, what treasure hast thou lost!
What face remains alive that's worth the viewing?
Whose tongue is music now? What canst thou boast
Of things long since, or any thing ensuing?   1078
  The flowers are sweet, their colors fresh and trim;
  But true sweet beauty lived and died with him.   *1080*

1059 *Dumbly . . . passions* she mimes grief; *doteth* gives way to folly   **1061**
bow bend   **1062** *are mad* go mad; *that . . . till now* that they have ever wept
before this moment   **1063** *steadfastly* fixedly   **1064** *dazzling* blurring
1065 *mangling* wounding   **1067** *several* separate   **1078** *ensuing* to come in
the future

"Bonnet nor veil henceforth no creature wear;
1082 Nor sun nor wind will ever strive to kiss you.
1083 Having no fair to lose, you need not fear;
The sun doth scorn you, and the wind doth hiss you.
     But when Adonis lived, sun and sharp air
     Lurked like two thieves to rob him of his fair;

"And therefore would he put his bonnet on,
1088 Under whose brim the gaudy sun would peep;
1089 The wind would blow it off, and, being gone,
1090 Play with his locks; then would Adonis weep;
     And straight, in pity of his tender years,
     They both would strive who first should dry his tears.

"To see his face the lion walked along
1094 Behind some hedge, because he would not fear him;
1095 To recreate himself when he hath sung,
The tiger would be tame and gently hear him;
     If he had spoke, the wolf would leave his prey,
1098 And never fright the silly lamb that day.

1099 "When he beheld his shadow in the brook,
1100 The fishes spread on it their golden gills;
When he was by, the birds such pleasure took
That some would sing, some other in their bills
     Would bring him mulberries and ripe-red cherries;
     He fed them with his sight, they him with berries.

1105 "But this foul, grim, and urchin-snouted boar,
1106 Whose downward eye still looketh for a grave,
1107 Ne'er saw the beauteous livery that he wore;

1082 *Nor . . . nor* neither . . . nor   1083 *fair* beauty, perfect complexion
1088 *gaudy* brilliant, sportive   1089 *being gone* it being gone   1094 *fear*
frighten   1095 *recreate* amuse   1098 *silly* helpless   1099 *shadow* reflection
1105 *urchin-snouted* with a snout like a hedgehog's   1106 *downward* down-
cast   1107 *livery* garb (i.e., his appearance)

Witness the entertainment that he gave.   1108
  If he did see his face, why then I know
  He thought to kiss him, and hath killed him so.   1110

"'Tis true, 'tis true; thus was Adonis slain:
He ran upon the boar with his sharp spear,   1112
Who did not whet his teeth at him again,   1113
But by a kiss thought to persuade him there;
  And nuzzling in his flank, the loving swine
  Sheathed unaware the tusk in his soft groin.

"Had I been toothed like him, I must confess,
With kissing him I should have killed him first;
But he is dead, and never did he bless   1119
My youth with his; the more am I accursed."   1120
  With this, she falleth in the place she stood,
  And stains her face with his congealèd blood.

She looks upon his lips, and they are pale;
She takes him by the hand, and that is cold;
She whispers in his ears a heavy tale,
As if they heard the woeful words she told;
  She lifts the coffer-lids that close his eyes,
  Where, lo, two lamps, burnt out, in darkness lies;

Two glasses where herself herself beheld
A thousand times, and now no more reflect,   1130
Their virtue lost wherein they late excelled,   1131
And every beauty robbed of his effect.
  "Wonder of time," quoth she, "this is my spite,   1133
  That, thou being dead, the day should yet be light.

"Since thou art dead, lo, here I prophesy
Sorrow on love hereafter shall attend:

1108 *entertainment* treatment **1112** *ran upon* attacked **1113** *whet*
sharpen; *again* in return **1119–20** *bless . . . his* leave me with a child **1131**
virtue power, quality **1133** *spite* punishing misfortune

1137 It shall be waited on with jealousy,
     Find sweet beginning but unsavory end;
1139 Ne'er settled equally, but high or low,
1140 That all love's pleasure shall not match his woe.

     "It shall be fickle, false, and full of fraud;
1142 Bud, and be blasted, in a breathing while;
1143 The bottom poison, and the top o'erstrawed
1144 With sweets that shall the truest sight beguile;
     The strongest body shall it make most weak,
     Strike the wise dumb, and teach the fool to speak.

1147 "It shall be sparing, and too full of riot,
1148 Teaching decrepit age to tread the measures;
1149 The staring ruffian shall it keep in quiet,
1150 Pluck down the rich, enrich the poor with treasures;
1151 It shall be raging-mad, and silly-mild,
     Make the young old, the old become a child.

     "It shall suspect where is no cause of fear;
     It shall not fear where it should most mistrust;
     It shall be merciful, and too severe,
     And most deceiving when it seems most just;
1157 Perverse it shall be where it shows most toward,
     Put fear to valor, courage to the coward.

     "It shall be cause of war and dire events,
1160 And set dissension 'twixt the son and sire;
1161 Subject and servile to all discontents,

1137 *waited on* attended by 1139 *settled equally* balanced, moderate 1142
a breathing while the space of a breath 1143 *o'erstrawed* strewn over 1144
sweets delights 1147 *sparing* abstinent, withholding; *riot* prodigal excess
1148 *tread the measures* dance; have intercourse ("tread") 1149 *staring* inso-
lent 1151 *silly* feebly 1157 *shows most toward* seems most attracted or
compliant 1161 *servile* at the service; *discontents* malcontents

As dry combustious matter is to fire.   1162
   Sith in his prime death doth my love destroy,
   They that love best their loves shall not enjoy."

By this the boy that by her side lay killed   1165
Was melted like a vapor from her sight,
And in his blood that on the ground lay spilled
A purple flower sprung up, checkered with white,   1168
   Resembling well his pale cheeks, and the blood
   Which in round drops upon their whiteness stood.   *1170*

She bows her head the new-sprung flower to smell,   1171
Comparing it to her Adonis' breath;
And says within her bosom it shall dwell,
Since he himself is reft from her by death.   1174
   She crops the stalk, and in the breach appears   1175
   Green-dropping sap, which she compares to tears.

"Poor flower," quoth she, "this was thy father's guise –   1177
Sweet issue of a more sweet-smelling sire –   1178
For every little grief to wet his eyes.
To grow unto himself was his desire,   1180
   And so 'tis thine; but know, it is as good
   To wither in my breast as in his blood.

"Here was thy father's bed, here in my breast;
Thou art the next of blood, and 'tis thy right.   1184
Lo, in this hollow cradle take thy rest;
My throbbing heart shall rock thee day and night;
   There shall not be one minute in an hour
   Wherein I will not kiss my sweet love's flower."

1162 *combustious* combustible   1165 *By this* by this time   1168 *checkered*
mottled   1171 *new-sprung* newly created or germinated   1174 *reft* stolen
1175 *crops* breaks off; *breach* break   1177 *guise* habit   1178 *issue* offspring
1180 *grow unto himself* be self-attached and self-propagating   1184 *next of
blood* lineal descendant

1189 Thus weary of the world, away she hies,
1190 And yokes her silver doves, by whose swift aid
       Their mistress, mounted, through the empty skies
       In her light chariot quickly is conveyed,
1193   Holding their course to Paphos, where their queen
1194   Means to immure herself and not be seen.

1189 *hies* hastens   1193 *Paphos* home of Venus   1194 *immure* cloister

Lucrece

TO THE
RIGHT HONORABLE
HENRY WRIOTHESLEY,
EARL OF SOUTHAMPTON AND BARON OF TITCHFIELD

The love I dedicate to your lordship is without end; whereof this pamphlet without beginning is but a super- 2 fluous moiety. The warrant I have of your honorable dis- 3 position, not the worth of my untutored lines, makes it assured of acceptance. What I have done is yours; what I have to do is yours; being part in all I have, devoted yours. 6 Were my worth greater, my duty would show greater; meantime, as it is, it is bound to your lordship, to whom I wish long life still lengthened with all happiness.

Your lordship's in all duty,
William Shakespeare

*

Dedication: Like *Venus and Adonis, Lucrece* is dedicated to the youthful Earl of Southampton, a noted literary patron. This dedication is more intimate and familiar than the previous one, implying Shakespeare's closer acquaintance with the earl.   **2** *pamphlet* short work; *without beginning* i.e., that plunges readers into the action   **3** *moiety* portion; *warrant* surety   **6** *have to do* have it in me to do; *devoted yours* wholly dedicated to you

Lucrece

THE ARGUMENT

Lucius Tarquinius, for his excessive pride surnamed Superbus, after he had caused his own father-in-law Servius Tullius to be cruelly murdered, and, contrary to the Roman laws and customs, not requiring or staying for the
5 people's suffrages, had possessed himself of the kingdom, went, accompanied with his sons and other noblemen of Rome, to besiege Ardea. During which siege, the principal men of the army meeting one evening at the tent of Sextus Tarquinius, the king's son, in their discourses after
10 supper everyone commended the virtues of his own wife; among whom Collatinus extolled the incomparable
12 chastity of his wife Lucretia. In that pleasant humor they
13 all posted to Rome; and intending, by their secret and sudden arrival, to make trial of that which everyone had
15 before avouched, only Collatinus finds his wife, though it were late in the night, spinning amongst her maids; the other ladies were all found dancing and reveling, or
18 in several disports. Whereupon the noblemen yielded Collatinus the victory and his wife the fame. At that time
20 Sextus Tarquinius, being inflamed with Lucrece' beauty, yet smothering his passions for the present, departed with

---

The Argument i.e., the plot and substance of the poem, derived from Livy's prose history of Rome from the foundation of the city, and the poet Ovid's *Fasti (Festivals)*. 5 *suffrages* votes 12 *pleasant humor* jocular mood 13 *posted* rode in haste 15 *avouched* affirmed 18 *disports* entertainments

the rest back to the camp; from whence he shortly after
privily withdrew himself, and was according to his estate   23
royally entertained and lodged by Lucrece at Collatium.
The same night he treacherously stealeth into her cham-
ber, violently ravished her, and early in the morning
speedeth away. Lucrece, in this lamentable plight, hastily
dispatcheth messengers, one to Rome for her father, an-
other to the camp for Collatine. They came, the one ac-
companied with Junius Brutus, the other with Publius   30
Valerius; and finding Lucrece attired in mourning habit,
demanded the cause of her sorrow. She, first taking an
oath of them for her revenge, revealed the actor and   33
whole manner of his dealing, and withal suddenly stabbed
herself. Which done, with one consent they all vowed to
root out the whole hated family of the Tarquins; and,
bearing the dead body to Rome, Brutus acquainted the
people with the doer and manner of the vile deed, with a
bitter invective against the tyranny of the king. Where-
with the people were so moved that with one consent and   40
a general acclamation the Tarquins were all exiled, and the
state government changed from kings to consuls.

*

From the besiegèd Ardea all in post,
Borne by the trustless wings of false desire,   2
Lust-breathèd Tarquin leaves the Roman host   3
And to Collatium bears the lightless fire   4
Which, in pale embers hid, lurks to aspire   5
   And girdle with embracing flames the waist   6
   Of Collatine's fair love, Lucrece the chaste.

---

23 *privily* secretly; *estate* rank   33 *actor* perpetrator   2 *trustless* untrustwor-
thy   3 *Lust-breathèd* animated by lust   4 *lightless fire* invisible flame (of his
desire)   5 *aspire* rise   6 *girdle* encircle

8 Haply the name of "chaste" unhapp'ly set
9 This bateless edge on his keen appetite,
10 When Collatine unwisely did not let
11 To praise the clear unmatchèd red and white
   Which triumphed in that sky of his delight,
13   Where mortal stars as bright as heaven's beauties
14   With pure aspects did him peculiar duties.

For he the night before in Tarquin's tent
Unlocked the treasure of his happy state;
What priceless wealth the heavens had him lent
In the possession of his beauteous mate;
19 Reckoning his fortune at such high-proud rate
20   That kings might be espousèd to more fame,
   But king nor peer to such a peerless dame.

O happiness enjoyed but of a few,
And, if possessed, as soon decayed and done
As is the morning silver melting dew
Against the golden splendor of the sun:
26 An expired date canceled ere well begun.
   Honor and beauty in the owner's arms
   Are weakly fortressed from a world of harms.

Beauty itself doth of itself persuade
30 The eyes of men without an orator;
31 What needeth then apology be made
32 To set forth that which is so singular?
33 Or why is Collatine the publisher
   Of that rich jewel he should keep unknown
   From thievish ears, because it is his own?

---

8 *Haply* perhaps; *unhapp'ly* unfortunately 9 *bateless* not to be blunted (abated) 10 *let* forbear 11 *red and white* (the facial complexion of the ideally beautiful woman in conventional Elizabethan love poetry) 13 *mortal stars* Lucrece's eyes 14 *pure aspects* clear, innocent looks; unobstructed visibility to the "earthly" observer; *peculiar* rendered to Collatine alone 19 *Reckoning* computing 26 *An expired . . . begun* i.e., contradictory reference to a document (e.g., a lease) either expired or prematurely canceled 31 *apology* justifying explanation (apologia) 32 *singular* unique and incomparable 33 *publisher* publicizer

Perchance his boast of Lucrece' sovereignty
Suggested this proud issue of a king;   37
For by our ears our hearts oft tainted be:
Perchance that envy of so rich a thing,
Braving compare, disdainfully did sting   40
   His high-pitched thoughts, that meaner men should 41
     vaunt
   That golden hap which their superiors want.   42

But some untimely thought did instigate
His all too timeless speed, if none of those;   44
His honor, his affairs, his friends, his state   45
Neglected all, with swift intent he goes
To quench the coal which in his liver glows.   47
   O rash false heat, wrapped in repentant cold,
   Thy hasty spring still blasts and ne'er grows old. 49

When at Collatium this false lord arrived,   50
Well was he welcomed by the Roman dame,
Within whose face beauty and virtue strived
Which of them both should underprop her fame: 53
When virtue bragged, beauty would blush for shame;
   When beauty boasted blushes, in despite   55
   Virtue would stain that o'er with silver white.

But beauty, in that white entitulèd   57
From Venus' doves, doth challenge that fair field;   58
Then virtue claims from beauty beauty's red,

---

37 *Suggested* tempted; *issue* offspring (i.e., Tarquin the younger) 40 *Braving compare* defying comparison; *disdainfully* slightingly 41 *high-pitched* ambitiously aspiring; *vaunt* boast 42 *hap* fortune; *want* lack 44 *timeless* hasty 45 *state* eminent position 47 *liver* (the organ believed in Elizabethan medicine to be the seat of the passions) 49 *still blasts* always withers 53 *underprop* support 55 *beauty . . . blushes* even beauty's modesty draws immodest attention to beauty by provoking an attractive blush; *in despite* in rivalrous antagonism 57 *in . . . entitulèd* legitimately possessed of 58 *challenge* lay claim to; *fair field* Lucrece's face

60 Which virtue gave the golden age to gild
61 Their silver cheeks, and called it then their shield;
      Teaching them thus to use it in the fight,
63   When shame assailed, the red should fence the white.

This heraldry in Lucrece' face was seen,
65 Argued by beauty's red and virtue's white;
Of either's color was the other queen,
67 Proving from world's minority their right;
Yet their ambition makes them still to fight,
69   The sovereignty of either being so great
70   That oft they interchange each other's seat.

This silent war of lilies and of roses
Which Tarquin viewed in her fair face's field
73 In their pure ranks his traitor eye encloses;
Where, lest between them both it should be killed,
The coward captive vanquishèd doth yield
      To those two armies that would let him go
77   Rather than triumph in so false a foe.

Now thinks he that her husband's shallow tongue,
79 The niggard prodigal that praised her so,
80 In that high task hath done her beauty wrong,
Which far exceeds his barren skill to show;
82 Therefore that praise which Collatine doth owe
83   Enchanted Tarquin answers with surmise,
      In silent wonder of still-gazing eyes.

This earthly saint adorèd by this devil
Little suspecteth the false worshiper;

60–61 *virtue . . . cheeks* virtue gave her red to tint pale silver into gold,
thereby creating a "golden age"; *shield* i.e., the perfect visage as defense
against shame   63 *fence* defend   65 *Argued* expressed   67 *world's minority*
the earliest times   69 *sovereignty* power to rule   70 *seat* place, throne   73
encloses either is enclosed by or inserts itself into   77 *in* both "over" and "in
the heart of"   79 *niggard prodigal* stingy spendthrift   82 *owe* i.e., still owes
in having fallen short   83 *answers . . . surmise* makes good by admiration

For unstained thoughts do seldom dream on evil;
Birds never limed no secret bushes fear:　　　　　　　　88
So, guiltless, she securely gives good cheer
　　And reverend welcome to her princely guest,　　　90
　　Whose inward ill no outward harm expressed.

For that he colored with his high estate,　　　　　　92
Hiding base sin in pleats of majesty,　　　　　　　　93
That nothing in him seemed inordinate　　　　　　　94
Save sometime too much wonder of his eye,
Which, having all, all could not satisfy;
　　But poorly rich so wanteth in his store　　　　　97
　　That cloyed with much he pineth still for more.

But she that never coped with stranger eyes　　　　99
Could pick no meaning from their parling looks,　100
Nor read the subtle shining secrecies　　　　　　　101
Writ in the glassy margents of such books:　　　　102
She touched no unknown baits; nor feared no hooks;　103
　　Nor could she moralize his wanton sight　　　　104
　　More than his eyes were opened to the light.　105

He stories to her ears her husband's fame,　　　　106
Won in the fields of fruitful Italy;
And decks with praises Collatine's high name,
Made glorious by his manly chivalry
With bruisèd arms and wreaths of victory.　　　　110
　　Her joy with heaved-up hand she doth express,　111
　　And wordless so greets heaven for his success.

---

88 *limed* trapped in birdlime; *secret* concealing (a snare)　90 *reverend* defer-
ential　92 *colored* disguised　93 *pleats* folds　94 *inordinate* out of the ordi-
nary, improper　97 *wanteth in his store* still lacks while having much　99
coped with confronted　100 *parling* speaking　101 *shining secrecies* evident
though "hidden" meanings　102 *glassy . . . books* i.e., she can't "read" the
marginal comments of his glances at her　103 *touched . . . baits* i.e., did not
touch the forms of bait she didn't even recognize　104 *moralize* interpret
morally　105 *More than* other than　106 *stories* relates, extols　110 *bruisèd*
dented　111 *heaved-up* upraised

Far from the purpose of his coming thither
He makes excuses for his being there.
No cloudy show of stormy blustering weather
116 Doth yet in his fair welkin once appear;
117 Till sable night, mother of dread and fear,
  Upon the world dim darkness doth display
  And in her vaulty prison stows the day.

120 For then is Tarquin brought unto his bed,
121 Intending weariness with heavy sprite;
122 For after supper long he questionèd
With modest Lucrece, and wore out the night.
Now leaden slumber with life's strength doth fight,
  And everyone to rest himself betakes,
  Save thieves and cares and troubled minds that wakes.

127 As one of which doth Tarquin lie revolving
The sundry dangers of his will's obtaining;
Yet ever to obtain his will resolving,
130 Though weak-built hopes persuade him to abstaining.
131 Despair to gain doth traffic oft for gaining,
132 And when great treasure is the meed proposed,
133 Though death be adjunct, there's no death supposed.

134 Those that much covet are with gain so fond
135 That what they have not, that which they possess,
They scatter and unloose it from their bond;
And so by hoping more they have but less,
Or gaining more, the profit of excess
139 Is but to surfeit, and such griefs sustain
140 That they prove bankrupt in this poor-rich gain.

---

116 *welkin* sky   117 *sable* black   121 *Intending* feigning; *sprite* spirit   122
questionèd conversed   127 *revolving* turning over in his mind   131 *traffic*
trade   132 *meed* reward   133 *adjunct* inseparably connected; *supposed*
imagined, conceived   134 *gain . . . fond* so infatuated with acquisition
135–36 *That . . . bond* i.e., they squander even what they possess to gain
more   139 *surfeit* sicken with excess; *sustain* suffer

The aim of all is but to nurse the life
With honor, wealth, and ease in waning age;
And in this aim there is such thwarting strife
That one for all or all for one we gage: 144
As life for honor in fell battle's rage;   145
   Honor for wealth; and oft that wealth doth cost
   The death of all, and all together lost.

So that in venturing ill we leave to be   148
The things we are for that which we expect;
And this ambitious foul infirmity   150
In having much torments us with defect   151
Of that we have; so then we do neglect
   The thing we have, and all for want of wit   153
   Make something nothing by augmenting it.

Such hazard now must doting Tarquin make,   155
Pawning his honor to obtain his lust;
And for himself himself he must forsake.   157
Then where is truth if there be no self-trust?
When shall he think to find a stranger just
   When he himself himself confounds, betrays   160
   To slanderous tongues and wretched hateful days?

Now stole upon the time the dead of night,
When heavy sleep had closed up mortal eyes;
No comfortable star did lend his light,   164
No noise but owls' and wolves' death-boding cries;   165
Now serves the season that they may surprise
   The silly lambs; pure thoughts are dead and still, 167
   While lust and murder wakes to stain and kill.

---

144 *gage* pledge, wager 145 *As* for example; *fell* deadly 148 *leave to be*
cease being 150 *infirmity* ailment, weakness 151 *defect* deficiency 153
wit reason 155 *hazard* gamble; *doting* desiring, foolish 157 *for . . . forsake*
for his own ends he must betray himself 160 *confounds* undoes 164 *com-
fortable* comforting 165 *death-boding* presaging death 167 *silly* feeble, in-
nocent

And now this lustful lord leaped from his bed,
170 Throwing his mantle rudely o'er his arm;
Is madly tossed between desire and dread:
Th' one sweetly flatters, th' other feareth harm;
173 But honest fear, bewitched with lust's foul charm,
     Doth too too oft betake him to retire,
175   Beaten away by brain-sick rude desire.

176 His falchion on a flint he softly smiteth,
That from the cold stone sparks of fire do fly;
Whereat a waxen torch forthwith he lighteth,
179 Which must be lodestar to his lustful eye;
180 And to the flame thus speaks advisedly:
     "As from this cold flint I enforced this fire,
     So Lucrece must I force to my desire."

183 Here pale with fear he doth premeditate
The dangers of his loathsome enterprise,
And in his inward mind he doth debate
186 What following sorrow may on this arise;
187 Then, looking scornfully, he doth despise
     His naked armor of still-slaughtered lust,
     And justly thus controls his thoughts unjust:

190 "Fair torch, burn out thy light, and lend it not
To darken her whose light excelleth thine;
192 And die, unhallowed thoughts, before you blot
With your uncleanness that which is divine;
Offer pure incense to so pure a shrine;
195   Let fair humanity abhor the deed
196   That spots and stains love's modest snow-white weed.

---

170 *rudely* inelegantly   173 *charm* magic spell   175 *brain-sick* i.e., compulsive, pathological; *rude* primitive   176 *falchion* sword   179 *lodestar* guiding star   180 *advisedly* with deliberation   183 *premeditate* anticipate in thought 186 *following* consequent 187–88 *he doth . . . lust* i.e., he views with disfavor the weakness of lust that dies in anticipation   192 *unhallowed* unsanctified 195 *abhor* regard with horror   196 *weed* garment

"O shame to knighthood and to shining arms!
O foul dishonor to my household's grave!   198
O impious act including all foul harms!
A martial man to be soft fancy's slave!   200
True valor still a true respect should have;
    Then my digression is so vile, so base,   202
    That it will live engraven in my face.

"Yea, though I die the scandal will survive
And be an eyesore in my golden coat:
Some loathsome dash the herald will contrive,   206
To cipher me how fondly I did dote,   207
That my posterity, shamed with the note,   208
    Shall curse my bones, and hold it for no sin
    To wish that I their father had not been.   210

"What win I if I gain the thing I seek?
A dream, a breath, a froth of fleeting joy.
Who buys a minute's mirth to wail a week?   213
Or sells eternity to get a toy?   214
For one sweet grape who will the vine destroy?
    Or what fond beggar, but to touch the crown,   216
    Would with the scepter straight be strucken down?

"If Collatinus dream of my intent,
Will he not wake, and in a desperate rage
Post hither, this vile purpose to prevent?   220
This siege that hath engirt his marriage,   221
This blur to youth, this sorrow to the sage,   222
    This dying virtue, this surviving shame,
    Whose crime will bear an ever-during blame.   224

---

198 *household's grave* family tomb   200 *fancy* imagination, desire   202 *digression* deviation   206 *dash* heraldic mark of shame   207 *cipher me* represent me   208 *note* mark   213 *mirth* laughter, pleasure   214 *toy* trifle   216 *fond* foolish   220 *Post* gallop   221 *engirt* encircled   222 *blur* blot; *the sage* the wise   224 *ever-during* eternal

"O what excuse can my invention make
When thou shalt charge me with so black a deed?
Will not my tongue be mute, my frail joints shake,
Mine eyes forgo their light, my false heart bleed?
The guilt being great, the fear doth still exceed;
230   And extreme fear can neither fight nor fly,
        But cowardlike with trembling terror die.

232 "Had Collatinus killed my son or sire,
Or lain in ambush to betray my life,
Or were he not my dear friend, this desire
235 Might have excuse to work upon his wife,
236 As in revenge or quittal of such strife;
        But as he is my kinsman, my dear friend,
        The shame and fault finds no excuse nor end.

"Shameful it is – ay, if the fact be known.
240 Hateful it is – there is no hate in loving.
241 I'll beg her love – but she is not her own.
The worst is but denial and reproving.
243 My will is strong past reason's weak removing:
244   Who fears a sentence or an old man's saw
245   Shall by a painted cloth be kept in awe."

246 Thus graceless holds he disputation
'Tween frozen conscience and hot-burning will,
248 And with good thoughts makes dispensation,
249 Urging the worser sense for vantage still;

---

232 *sire* father   235 *work upon* undermine, have sex with   236 *quittal* re-
quital   241 *her own* i.e., a free agent   243 *will* determination, sexual im-
pulse; *past . . . removing* beyond reason's weak control   244 *sentence* moral
maxim; *saw* trite saying   245 *painted cloth* pictorial wall hanging, conveying
a moral message   246 *graceless* ungracefully, without the help of divine grace
248 *good . . . dispensation* "dispenses with good thoughts" or "gains sanction
through the process of reasoning"   249 *Urging . . . still* i.e., striving to place
the worst possibility in the best light

Which in a moment doth confound and kill   *250*
  All pure effects, and doth so far proceed   *251*
  That what is vile shows like a virtuous deed.

Quoth he, "She took me kindly by the hand,
And gazed for tidings in my eager eyes,
Fearing some hard news from the warlike band
Where her belovèd Collatinus lies.
O how her fear did make her color rise!
  First red as roses that on lawn we lay,   *258*
  Then white as lawn, the roses took away.

"And how her hand in my hand being locked   *260*
Forced it to tremble with her loyal fear!
Which struck her sad, and then it faster rocked   *262*
Until her husband's welfare she did hear;
Whereat she smilèd with so sweet a cheer   *264*
  That had Narcissus seen her as she stood
  Self-love had never drowned him in the flood.

"Why hunt I then for color or excuses?   *267*
All orators are dumb when beauty pleadeth;
Poor wretches have remorse in poor abuses;   *269*
Love thrives not in the heart that shadows dreadeth;   *270*
Affection is my captain, and he leadeth;   *271*
  And when his gaudy banner is displayed
  The coward fights and will not be dismayed.   *273*

"Then childish fear avaunt, debating die!   *274*
Respect and reason wait on wrinkled age!
My heart shall never countermand mine eye;
Sad pause and deep regard beseems the sage: *277*

---

251 *effects* thoughts and feelings   **258** *lawn* fine linen   **262** *it* her heart (?);
rocked beat   **264** *cheer* good cheer   **267** *color* pretext, specious justification
269 *Poor . . . abuses* feeble persons feel compunction for slight offenses   **270**
shadows (daunting) images   **271** *Affection* desire   **273** *The coward fights* i.e.,
even the coward fights   **274** *avaunt* be gone   **277** *Sad pause* sober hesita-
tion; *deep regard* profound reflection; *beseems* befits

My part is youth, and beats these from the stage.
   Desire my pilot is, beauty my prize;
280   Then who fears sinking where such treasure lies?"

281 As corn o'ergrown by weeds, so heedful fear
Is almost choked by unresisted lust.
Away he steals with open listening ear,
284 Full of foul hope and full of fond mistrust;
285 Both which, as servitors to the unjust,
286   So cross him with their opposite persuasion
287   That now he vows a league, and now invasion.

Within his thought her heavenly image sits,
And in the selfsame seat sits Collatine.
290 That eye which looks on her confounds his wits;
291 That eye which him beholds, as more divine,
Unto a view so false will not incline;
   But with a pure appeal seeks to the heart,
   Which once corrupted takes the worser part;

295 And therein heartens up his servile powers,
296 Who, flattered by their leader's jocund show,
Stuff up his lust, as minutes fill up hours;
298 And as their captain, so their pride doth grow,
Paying more slavish tribute than they owe.
300   By reprobate desire thus madly led
   The Roman lord marcheth to Lucrece' bed.

The locks between her chamber and his will,
303 Each one by him enforced, retires his ward;
304 But as they open, they all rate his ill,

---

281 *heedful* cautious 284 *mistrust* uncertainty, misgiving 285 *servitors* attendants 286 *cross* "confuse" or "contradict" 287 *league* truce, peace 291 *as* being 295 *servile powers* senses and bodily functions 296 *jocund* high-spirited 298 *as* like; *their captain* i.e., the heart 300 *reprobate* unholy, wicked 303 *enforced* forced; *ward* metal plate that prevents the lock from being turned by any key except the right one 304 *rate* scold (by creaking)

Which drives the creeping thief to some regard.   305
The threshold grates the door to have him heard;   306
  Night-wandering weasels shriek to see him there;
  They fright him, yet he still pursues his fear.   308

As each unwilling portal yields him way,   309
Through little vents and crannies of the place   *310*
The wind wars with his torch to make him stay,   311
And blows the smoke of it into his face,
Extinguishing his conduct in this case;   313
  But his hot heart, which fond desire doth scorch,
  Puffs forth another wind that fires the torch.   315

And being lighted, by the light he spies
Lucretia's glove, wherein her needle sticks;
He takes it from the rushes where it lies,
And gripping it, the needle his finger pricks,
As who should say "This glove to wanton tricks   320
  Is not inured; return again in haste;   321
  Thou seest our mistress' ornaments are chaste."

But all these poor forbiddings could not stay him;
He in the worst sense consters their denial: 324
The doors, the wind, the glove, that did delay him
He takes for accidental things of trial;   326
Or as those bars which stop the hourly dial,   327
  Who with a lingering stay his course doth let   328
  Till every minute pays the hour his debt.

---

305 *regard* caution   306 *to have him heard* so that he may be heard   308 *his
fear* that which he fears to do   309 *portal* doorway   311 *stay* stop   313 *con-
duct* guide   315 *fires* reignites   320 *As . . . say* as one who would say   321
inured accustomed   324 *consters* construes   326 *accidental . . . trial* chance
obstacles to be overcome   327 *those . . . dial* the marks on a clock face at
which the hands appear to pause   328 *Who* which; *his* its; *let* arrest

330 "So, so," quoth he, "these lets attend the time,
Like little frosts that sometime threat the spring,
332 To add a more rejoicing to the prime
333 And give the sneapèd birds more cause to sing.
334 Pain pays the income of each precious thing:
    Huge rocks, high winds, strong pirates, shelves, and sands
    The merchant fears, ere rich at home he lands."

Now is he come unto the chamber door
338 That shuts him from the heaven of his thought,
Which with a yielding latch, and with no more,
340 Hath barred him from the blessèd thing he sought.
341 So from himself impiety hath wrought
342   That for his prey to pray he doth begin,
    As if the heavens should countenance his sin.

But in the midst of his unfruitful prayer,
Having solicited th' eternal power
346 That his foul thoughts might compass his fair fair,
And they would stand auspicious to the hour,
348 Even there he starts; quoth he, "I must deflower:
    The powers to whom I pray abhor this fact;
350   How can they then assist me in the act?

"Then love and fortune be my gods, my guide!
352 My will is backed with resolution;
353 Thoughts are but dreams till their effects be tried;
The blackest sin is cleared with absolution;
Against love's fire fear's frost hath dissolution.
356   The eye of heaven is out, and misty night
    Covers the shame that follows sweet delight."

---

330 *lets* pauses; *attend* wait upon   332 *prime* spring   333 *sneapèd* pinched
with the cold   334 *pays* is the cost of; *income* attainment   338 *heaven . . .
thought* the heaven he imagines   341 *from himself* away from his true or bet-
ter self; *wrought* worked (to remove him)   342 *prey* i.e., his successful con-
quest of Lucrece   346 *compass* encompass   348 *starts* recoils   352 *will*
desire   353 *effects* results in action   356 *out* extinguished, blinded

This said, his guilty hand plucked up the latch,
And with his knee the door he opens wide.
The dove sleeps fast that this night owl will catch;　　　　360
Thus treason works ere traitors be espied.
Who sees the lurking serpent steps aside;
　　But she, sound sleeping, fearing no such thing,
　　Lies at the mercy of his mortal sting.　　　　364

Into the chamber wickedly he stalks,
And gazeth on her yet unstainèd bed.
The curtains being close, about he walks,
Rolling his greedy eyeballs in his head;
By their high treason is his heart misled,
　　Which gives the watchword to his hand full soon　　　　370
　　To draw the cloud that hides the silver moon.

Look as the fair and fiery-pointed sun
Rushing from forth a cloud bereaves our sight,　　　　373
Even so, the curtain drawn, his eyes begun
To wink, being blinded with a greater light.　　　　375
Whether it is that she reflects so bright
　　That dazzleth them, or else some shame supposed,　　　　377
　　But blind they are, and keep themselves enclosed.

O, had they in that darksome prison died,　　　　379
Then had they seen the period of their ill;　　　　380
Then Collatine again by Lucrece' side
In his clear bed might have reposèd still.　　　　382
But they must ope, this blessèd league to kill;　　　　383
　　And holy-thoughted Lucrece to their sight
　　Must sell her joy, her life, her world's delight.

---

364 *mortal* deadly; *sting* bite　370 *watchword* signal to attack　373
bereaves . . . sight deprives us of sight　375 *wink* blink　377 *supposed* imag-
ined　379 *had* if only they had　380 *had* would have; *period* ending　382
clear unstained　383 *ope* open; *blessèd league* i.e., the marriage

Her lily hand her rosy cheek lies under,
387 Cozening the pillow of a lawful kiss;
388 Who therefore angry seems to part in sunder,
389 Swelling on either side to want his bliss;
390 Between whose hills her head entombèd is;
391   Where like a virtuous monument she lies
392   To be admired of lewd unhallowed eyes.

393 Without the bed her other fair hand was,
On the green coverlet, whose perfect white
Showed like an April daisy on the grass,
With pearly sweat resembling dew of night.
Her eyes like marigolds had sheathed their light,
    And canopied in darkness sweetly lay
    Till they might open to adorn the day.

400 Her hair like golden threads played with her breath:
O modest wantons, wanton modesty!
402 Showing life's triumph in the map of death,
403 And death's dim look in life's mortality:
404 Each in her sleep themselves so beautify
    As if between them twain there were no strife,
    But that life lived in death and death in life.

Her breasts like ivory globes circled with blue,
A pair of maiden worlds unconquerèd,
Save of their lord no bearing yoke they knew,
410 And him by oath they truly honorèd.
These worlds in Tarquin new ambition bred,
    Who like a foul usurper went about
    From this fair throne to heave the owner out.

---

387 *Cozening* cheating   388 *part in sunder* i.e., be separated from or divided   389 *Swelling* i.e., in anger; *want* lack   391 *virtuous monument* tomb sculpture portraying the virtue of the dead person   392 *admired of* wondered at   393 *Without* outside   402 *map* image, picture   403 *life's mortality* i.e., in the mortal, living person   404 *beautify* i.e., present themselves beautifully

What could he see but mightily he noted?
What did he note but strongly he desired?
What he beheld, on that he firmly doted,
And in his will his willful eye he tired.   417
With more than admiration he admired   418
  Her azure veins, her alabaster skin,   419
  Her coral lips, her snow-white dimpled chin.   420

As the grim lion fawneth o'er his prey,   421
Sharp hunger by the conquest satisfied,
So o'er this sleeping soul doth Tarquin stay,   423
His rage of lust by gazing qualified: 424
Slacked not suppressed; for standing by her side,
  His eye which late this mutiny restrains   426
  Upon a greater uproar tempts his veins.

And they like straggling slaves for pillage fighting,   428
Obdurate vassals fell exploits effecting,   429
In bloody death and ravishment delighting,   430
Nor children's tears nor mothers' groans respecting,
Swell in their pride, the onset still expecting.
  Anon his beating heart, alarum striking,   433
  Gives the hot charge, and bids them do their liking.   434

His drumming heart cheers up his burning eye,   435
His eye commends the leading to his hand;   436
His hand, as proud of such a dignity,   437
Smoking with pride, marched on to make his stand   438

---

417 *tired* both "attired" and "fatigued"   418 *more . . . admired* i.e., with lust
rather than pure wonder   419 *azure* blue   421 *fawneth* affectionately gazes
423 *stay* pause   424 *qualified* softened   426 *this mutiny* i.e., the revolt of
lust against reason   428 *straggling slaves* camp followers; *pillage* spoils   429
Obdurate . . . effecting i.e., base, ruthless stragglers doing terrible deeds   433
alarum drum-roll call to arms   434 *charge* order to charge   435 *cheers up*
heartens   436 *commends* delegates   437 *as* as if   438 *Smoking* i.e., over-
heated

On her bare breast, the heart of all her land;
440   Whose ranks of blue veins, as his hand did scale,
       Left their round turrets destitute and pale.

442 They, mustering to the quiet cabinet
     Where their dear governess and lady lies,
     Do tell her she is dreadfully beset,
     And fright her with confusion of their cries.
446 She much amazed breaks ope her locked-up eyes,
       Who, peeping forth this tumult to behold,
448   Are by his flaming torch dimmed and controlled.

     Imagine her as one in dead of night
450 From forth dull sleep by dreadful fancy waking,
451 That thinks she hath beheld some ghastly sprite
452 Whose grim aspect sets every joint a-shaking;
453 What terror 'tis! but she in worser taking,
454   From sleep disturbèd, heedfully doth view
455   The sight which makes supposèd terror true.

     Wrapped and confounded in a thousand fears,
     Like to a new-killed bird she trembling lies;
458 She dares not look, yet, winking, there appears
459 Quick-shifting antics, ugly in her eyes.
460 Such shadows are the weak brain's forgeries,
461   Who, angry that the eyes fly from their lights,
       In darkness daunts them with more dreadful sights.

     His hand that yet remains upon her breast –
464 Rude ram, to batter such an ivory wall –

---

440 *scale* mount   442 *mustering to* gathering in; *cabinet* i.e., her heart (?)
446 *ope* open   448 *controlled* subjugated   450 *dreadful fancy* terrifying
image (as in a nightmare)   451 *ghastly sprite* fearful, ghostly apparition
452 *aspect* appearance   453 *taking* state of dread   454 *heedfully* in full con-
sciousness   455 *supposèd* imagined   458 *winking* with eyes closed   459
Quick-shifting antics rapidly changing grotesque images   460 *shadows* im-
ages   461 *fly . . . lights* abandon their task of vision   464 *Rude* both "un-
couth" and "brutal"

May feel her heart, poor citizen, distressed,
Wounding itself to death, rise up and fall,
Beating her bulk, that his hand shakes withal.   467
    This moves in him more rage and lesser pity
    To make the breach and enter this sweet city.

First like a trumpet doth his tongue begin   470
To sound a parley to his heartless foe,   471
Who o'er the white sheet peers her whiter chin,
The reason of this rash alarm to know,
Which he by dumb demeanor seeks to show;
    But she with vehement prayers urgeth still
    Under what color he commits this ill.   476

Thus he replies: "The color in thy face,
That even for anger makes the lily pale
And the red rose blush at her own disgrace,
Shall plead for me and tell my loving tale.   480
Under that color am I come to scale
    Thy never-conquered fort: the fault is thine,
    For those thine eyes betray thee unto mine.

"Thus I forestall thee, if thou mean to chide:
Thy beauty hath ensnared thee to this night,
Where thou with patience must my will abide,
My will that marks thee for my earth's delight,
Which I to conquer sought with all my might;
    But as reproof and reason beat it dead,
    By thy bright beauty was it newly bred.   490

"I see what crosses my attempt will bring;   491
I know what thorns the growing rose defends;
I think the honey guarded with a sting;
All this beforehand counsel comprehends.   494

---

467 *bulk* chest wall   471 *parley* call to negotiate terms; *heartless* disheart-
ened, fearful   476 *color* pretext   491 *crosses* adversities   494 *counsel* reason

495 But will is deaf, and hears no heedful friends;
    Only he hath an eye to gaze on beauty,
    And dotes on what he looks, 'gainst law or duty.

"I have debated even in my soul
What wrong, what shame, what sorrow I shall breed;
500 But nothing can affection's course control,
Or stop the headlong fury of his speed.
I know repentant tears ensue the deed,
    Reproach, disdain, and deadly enmity;
    Yet strive I to embrace mine infamy."

This said, he shakes aloft his Roman blade,
Which like a falcon towering in the skies
507 Coucheth the fowl below with his wings' shade,
508 Whose crooked beak threats if he mount he dies.
509 So under his insulting falchion lies
510   Harmless Lucretia, marking what he tells
511   With trembling fear, as fowl hear falcons' bells.

"Lucrece," quoth he, "this night I must enjoy thee.
If thou deny, then force must work my way,
514 For in thy bed I purpose to destroy thee;
That done, some worthless slave of thine I'll slay,
516 To kill thine honor with thy life's decay;
    And in thy dead arms do I mean to place him,
    Swearing I slew him, seeing thee embrace him.

"So thy surviving husband shall remain
520 The scornful mark of every open eye;
521 Thy kinsmen hang their heads at this disdain,
522 Thy issue blurred with nameless bastardy;

---

495 *heedful* cautious   500 *affection* sexual desire   507 *Coucheth* causes to
cower   508 *threats* threatens   509 *insulting falchion* insolently threatening
sword   510 *marking* attending to   511 *fowl* birds; *falcons' bells* bells tied to
trained birds of prey to enable hunters to locate them   514 *purpose* intend
516 *decay* loss   520 *mark* object   521 *disdain* disgrace   522 *issue* progeny;
blurred blemished; *nameless bastardy* i.e., of low, unidentifiable paternity

And thou, the author of their obloquy,   523
　　Shalt have thy trespass cited up in rhymes   524
　　And sung by children in succeeding times.

"But if thou yield, I rest thy secret friend;   526
The fault unknown is as a thought unacted;
A little harm done to a great good end
For lawful policy remains enacted;   529
The poisonous simple sometime is compacted   530
　　In a pure compound; being so applied,
　　His venom in effect is purified.

"Then for thy husband and thy children's sake,
Tender my suit; bequeath not to their lot
The shame that from them no device can take,   535
The blemish that will never be forgot,
Worse than a slavish wipe or birth-hour's blot;   537
　　For marks descried in men's nativity   538
　　Are nature's faults, not their own infamy."

Here with a cockatrice' dead-killing eye   540
He rouseth up himself, and makes a pause;
While she, the picture of pure piety,
Like a white hind under the gripe's sharp claws,   543
Pleads in a wilderness where are no laws
　　To the rough beast that knows no gentle right,   545
　　Nor aught obeys but his foul appetite.

But when a black-faced cloud the world doth threat,
In his dim mist th' aspiring mountains hiding,   548
From earth's dark womb some gentle gust doth get,   549

---

523 *author* cause; *obloquy* shame   524 *cited up* commemorated   526 *rest* remain; *secret friend* lover, secret-sharer   529 *For . . . enacted* is sanctioned as legitimate   530 *simple* drug; *compacted* combined   535 *device* contrivance   537 *wipe* brand (?); *birth-hour's blot* disfiguring birthmark   538 *descried* observed   540 *cockatrice* mythical creature that kills with a look   543 *hind* female deer; *gripe* mythical predator, bird of prey   545 *gentle right* chivalrous code, civil regulation   548 *th' aspiring* upraised   549 *get* beget

550 Which blow these pitchy vapors from their biding,
551 Hindering their present fall by this dividing;
    So his unhallowed haste her words delays,
553   And moody Pluto winks while Orpheus plays.

Yet, foul night-waking cat, he doth but dally
While in his hold-fast foot the weak mouse panteth;
556 Her sad behavior feeds his vulture folly,
A swallowing gulf that even in plenty wanteth;
His ear her prayers admits, but his heart granteth
559   No penetrable entrance to her plaining:
560   Tears harden lust, though marble wear with raining.

Her pity-pleading eyes are sadly fixed
562 In the remorseless wrinkles of his face;
Her modest eloquence with sighs is mixed,
Which to her oratory adds more grace.
565 She puts the period often from his place,
    And 'midst the sentence so her accent breaks
    That twice she doth begin ere once she speaks.

568 She conjures him by high almighty Jove,
569 By knighthood, gentry, and sweet friendship's oath,
570 By her untimely tears, her husband's love,
571 By holy human law and common troth,
By heaven and earth, and all the power of both,
    That to his borrowed bed he make retire,
    And stoop to honor, not to foul desire.

Quoth she, "Reward not hospitality
576 With such black payment as thou hast pretended;

---

550 *biding* place   551 *present fall* immediate downpour; *this* them   553
moody Pluto depressed, angry king of the underworld; *winks* sleeps; *Orpheus*
(legendary singer, whose music charmed Pluto into releasing his dead wife,
Eurydice, from the underworld)   556 *sad* sober   559 *plaining* lamenting
562 *wrinkles* i.e., frown   565 *puts . . . place* breaks off in mid-sentence   568
conjures implores   569 *gentry* noble birth   570 *untimely* unfitting   571
troth honesty   576 *pretended* offered

Mud not the fountain that gave drink to thee;
Mar not the thing that cannot be amended;
End thy ill aim before thy shoot be ended;   579
    He is no woodman that doth bend his bow   580
    To strike a poor unseasonable doe.   581

"My husband is thy friend; for his sake spare me:
Thyself art mighty; for thine own sake leave me:
Myself a weakling; do not then ensnare me:
Thou look'st not like deceit; do not deceive me.
My sighs like whirlwinds labor hence to heave thee.
    If ever man were moved with woman's moans,
    Be movèd with my tears, my sighs, my groans:

"All which together, like a troubled ocean,
Beat at thy rocky and wrack-threatening heart,   590
To soften it with their continual motion;
For stones dissolved to water do convert.   592
O, if no harder than a stone thou art,
    Melt at my tears and be compassionate;
    Soft pity enters at an iron gate.

"In Tarquin's likeness I did entertain thee:
Hast thou put on his shape to do him shame?
To all the host of heaven I complain me
Thou wrong'st his honor, wound'st his princely name:
Thou art not what thou seem'st; and if the same,   600
    Thou seem'st not what thou art, a god, a king;
    For kings like gods should govern everything.   602

"How will thy shame be seeded in thine age,   603
When thus thy vices bud before thy spring?
If in thy hope thou dar'st do such outrage,   605

---

579 *shoot* bow shot   580 *woodman* huntsman   581 *unseasonable* out of season   590 *wrack* wreck   592 *do convert* change into   602 *govern everything* remain in control of everything, including themselves   603 *be seeded* increase and multiply   605 *hope* expectation (of kingship)

What dar'st thou not when once thou art a king?
607 O, be remembered, no outrageous thing
608   From vassal actors can be wiped away;
609   Then kings' misdeeds cannot be hid in clay.

610 "This deed will make thee only loved for fear,
    But happy monarchs still are feared for love;
612 With foul offenders thou perforce must bear,
    When they in thee the like offenses prove.
614 If but for fear of this, thy will remove;
615   For princes are the glass, the school, the book,
     Where subjects' eyes do learn, do read, do look.

"And wilt thou be the school where lust shall learn?
618 Must he in thee read lectures of such shame?
    Wilt thou be glass wherein it shall discern
620 Authority for sin, warrant for blame,
    To privilege dishonor in thy name?
622   Thou back'st reproach against long-living laud,
623   And mak'st fair reputation but a bawd.

"Hast thou command? By him that gave it thee,
    From a pure heart command thy rebel will.
    Draw not thy sword to guard iniquity,
627 For it was lent thee all that brood to kill.
    Thy princely office how canst thou fulfill,
629   When patterned by thy fault foul sin may say
630   He learned to sin, and thou didst teach the way?

"Think but how vile a spectacle it were
To view thy present trespass in another.
Men's faults do seldom to themselves appear;

---

607 *remembered* reminded   608 *vassal actors* socially inferior transgressors
609 *in clay* after burial   612 *perforce must bear* will have to tolerate   614
but only; *remove* detach (from me)   615 *glass* mirror   618 *he* the subject
620 *blame* culpable conduct   622 *back'st* bet on; *laud* praise   623 *bawd*
pimp   627 *all that brood* that entire breed   629 *patterned* given a model

Their own transgressions partially they smother.   634
This guilt would seem death-worthy in thy brother.
   O, how are they wrapped in with infamies   636
   That from their own misdeeds askance their eyes!   637

"To thee, to thee, my heaved-up hands appeal,   638
Not to seducing lust, thy rash relier: 639
I sue for exiled majesty's repeal;   640
Let him return, and flattering thoughts retire:
His true respect will prison false desire,   642
   And wipe the dim mist from thy doting eyne,   643
   That thou shalt see thy state, and pity mine."   644

"Have done," quoth he, "my uncontrollèd tide
Turns not, but swells the higher by this let.   646
Small lights are soon blown out; huge fires abide,
And with the wind in greater fury fret;   648
The petty streams that pay a daily debt
   To their salt sovereign, with their fresh falls' haste   650
   Add to his flow, but alter not his taste."

"Thou art," quoth she, "a sea, a sovereign king,
And lo, there falls into thy boundless flood
Black lust, dishonor, shame, misgoverning,
Who seek to stain the ocean of thy blood.   655
If all these petty ills shall change thy good,
   Thy sea within a puddle's womb is hearsed,   657
   And not the puddle in thy sea dispersed.

---

634 *partially they smother* conceal from themselves out of partiality 636
wrapped involved 637 *askance* avert 638 *heaved-up* upraised 639 *relier*
source of reliance 640 *sue* plead; *repeal* recall from exile 642 *prison* im-
prison 643 *eyne* eyes 644 *state* condition 646 *let* obstacle 648 *fret* rage
650 *salt sovereign* the ocean; *falls'* rapids' 655 *Who* which 657 *Thy . . .
hearsed* i.e., your sea is both confined and interred in the space of a puddle

659 "So shall these slaves be king, and thou their slave;
660 Thou nobly base, they basely dignified;
Thou their fair life, and they thy fouler grave;
Thou loathèd in their shame, they in thy pride.
The lesser thing should not the greater hide:
    The cedar stoops not to the base shrub's foot,
    But low shrubs wither at the cedar's root.

666 "So let thy thoughts, low vassals to thy state" –
"No more," quoth he, "by heaven I will not hear thee.
668 Yield to my love; if not, enforcèd hate
669 Instead of love's coy touch shall rudely tear thee.
670 That done, despitefully I mean to bear thee
    Unto the base bed of some rascal groom,
    To be thy partner in this shameful doom."

This said, he sets his foot upon the light,
For light and lust are deadly enemies:
Shame folded up in blind concealing night,
When most unseen, then most doth tyrannize.
The wolf hath seized his prey, the poor lamb cries,
678   Till with her own white fleece her voice controlled
    Entombs her outcry in her lips' sweet fold.

680 For with the nightly linen that she wears
681 He pens her piteous clamors in her head,
Cooling his hot face in the chastest tears
That ever modest eyes with sorrow shed.
684 O, that prone lust should stain so pure a bed!
    The spots whereof could weeping purify,
    Her tears should drop on them perpetually.

---

659 *these slaves* i.e., evils   **666** *low vassals . . . state* lowly servants to your
high condition   **668** *enforcèd hate* hate backed up by action   **669** *coy* tender
670 *despitefully* with malicious cruelty   **678** *controlled* silenced   **681** *pens*
gags   **684** *prone* eager, lying face downward

But she hath lost a dearer thing than life,
And he hath won what he would lose again.   688
This forcèd league doth force a further strife;   689
This momentary joy breeds months of pain;   690
This hot desire converts to cold disdain;
    Pure chastity is rifled of her store,
    And lust the thief far poorer than before.

Look as the full-fed hound or gorgèd hawk,   694
Unapt for tender smell or speedy flight,   695
Make slow pursuit, or altogether balk   696
The prey wherein by nature they delight,
So surfeit-taking Tarquin fares this night;   698
    His taste delicious, in digestion souring,
    Devours his will that lived by foul devouring.   700

O deeper sin than bottomless conceit   701
Can comprehend in still imagination!   702
Drunken desire must vomit his receipt   703
Ere he can see his own abomination.
While lust is in his pride, no exclamation
    Can curb his heat or rein his rash desire,
    Till, like a jade, self-will himself doth tire.   707

And then with lank and lean discolored cheek,   708
With heavy eye, knit brow, and strengthless pace,
Feeble desire, all recreant, poor, and meek,   710
Like to a bankrupt beggar wails his case.
The flesh being proud, desire doth fight with grace;
    For there it revels, and when that decays,   713
    The guilty rebel for remission prays.   714

---

688 *would lose* would want to lose   **689** *forcèd league* forced union   **694** *gorgèd* satiated   **695** *Unapt* unfit, disinclined   **696** *balk* let go   **698** *surfeit-taking* taking pleasure to excess   **700** *Devours his will* consumes his own desire   **701** *conceit* thought   **702** *still* i.e., sober   **703** *his receipt* what it has consumed   **707** *jade* worn-out horse   **708** *lank* shrunken   **710** *recreant* cowardly   **713** *there* i.e., in the flesh   **714** *remission* pardon, absolution

So fares it with this faultful lord of Rome,
Who this accomplishment so hotly chased;
717 For now against himself he sounds this doom,
That through the length of times he stands disgraced.
Besides, his soul's fair temple is defaced,
720   To whose weak ruins muster troops of cares
721   To ask the spotted princess how she fares.

She says her subjects with foul insurrection
723 Have battered down her consecrated wall,
And by their mortal fault brought in subjection
725 Her immortality, and made her thrall
To living death and pain perpetual;
727   Which in her prescience she controllèd still,
        But her foresight could not forestall their will.

Even in this thought through the dark night he stealeth,
730 A captive victor that hath lost in gain;
Bearing away the wound that nothing healeth,
The scar that will, despite of cure, remain;
733 Leaving his spoil perplexed in greater pain.
        She bears the load of lust he left behind,
        And he the burden of a guilty mind.

He like a thievish dog creeps sadly thence;
She like a wearied lamb lies panting there;
He scowls, and hates himself for his offense;
She, desperate, with her nails her flesh doth tear.
740 He faintly flies, sweating with guilty fear;
741   She stays, exclaiming on the direful night;
        He runs, and chides his vanished loathed delight.

---

717 *sounds this doom* passes judgment   720 *muster* assemble   721 *spotted
princess* i.e., his besmirched soul   723 *consecrated* holy   725 *thrall* bondslave
727 *controllèd* governed   733 *his spoil* i.e., Lucrece   740 *faintly* fearfully
741 *direful* dreadful

He thence departs a heavy convertite;   743
She there remains a hopeless castaway;
He in his speed looks for the morning light;
She prays she never may behold the day.
"For day," quoth she, "night's scapes doth open lay,   747
    And my true eyes have never practiced how
    To cloak offenses with a cunning brow.

"They think not but that every eye can see   750
The same disgrace which they themselves behold;
And therefore would they still in darkness be,   752
To have their unseen sin remain untold.
For they their guilt with weeping will unfold,
    And grave, like water that doth eat in steel,   755
    Upon my cheeks what helpless shame I feel."

Here she exclaims against repose and rest,
And bids her eyes hereafter still be blind;   758
She wakes her heart by beating on her breast,
And bids it leap from thence, where it may find   760
Some purer chest to close so pure a mind.   761
    Frantic with grief thus breathes she forth her spite
    Against the unseen secrecy of night:

"O comfort-killing night, image of hell,
Dim register and notary of shame,   765
Black stage for tragedies and murders fell,   766
Vast sin-concealing chaos, nurse of blame!
Blind muffled bawd, dark harbor for defame,   768
    Grim cave of death, whispering conspirator
    With close-tongued treason and the ravisher!   770

---

743 *heavy convertite* sad penitent   747 *scapes* guilty acts   750 *They* her eyes;
think not but that think only that   752 *would* would want   755 *grave* en-
grave; *water . . . steel* i.e., acid   758 *still* forever   761 *close* enclose   765 *reg-
ister* record book; *notary* recorder   766 *fell* cruel   768 *bawd* pimp; *defame*
infamy   770 *close-tongued* secretive

"O hateful, vaporous, and foggy night,
Since thou art guilty of my cureless crime,
Muster thy mists to meet the eastern light,
774 Make war against proportioned course of time;
Or if thou wilt permit the sun to climb
776   His wonted height, yet ere he go to bed
    Knit poisonous clouds about his golden head.

"With rotten damps ravish the morning air;
Let their exhaled unwholesome breaths make sick
780 The life of purity, the supreme fair,
781 Ere he arrive his weary noontide prick;
And let thy musty vapors march so thick
    That in their smoky ranks his smothered light
    May set at noon and make perpetual night.

"Were Tarquin night, as he is but night's child,
786 The silver-shining queen he would distain;
787 Her twinkling handmaids too, by him defiled,
Through night's black bosom should not peep again.
So should I have co-partners in my pain;
790   And fellowship in woe doth woe assuage,
791   As palmers' chat makes short their pilgrimage.

"Where now I have no one to blush with me,
To cross their arms and hang their heads with mine,
794 To mask their brows and hide their infamy;
But I alone alone must sit and pine,
796 Seasoning the earth with showers of silver brine,
    Mingling my talk with tears, my grief with groans,
798   Poor wasting monuments of lasting moans.

---

774 *proportioned* regular   776 *wonted* accustomed   780 *The . . . fair* i.e.,
the sun   781 *prick* mark on the dial   786 *silver-shining queen* the moon;
distain defile   787 *handmaids* i.e., the stars   791 *palmers* pilgrims to the
Holy Land   794 *mask their brows* cover their faces   796 *brine* salt water
798 *wasting monuments* transitory memorials

"O night, thou furnace of foul reeking smoke,
Let not the jealous day behold that face   800
Which underneath thy black all-hiding cloak
Immodestly lies martyred with disgrace!
Keep still possession of thy gloomy place,   803
   That all the faults which in thy reign are made
   May likewise be sepulchered in thy shade.   805

"Make me not object to the telltale day: 806
The light will show charactered in my brow   807
The story of sweet chastity's decay,
The impious breach of holy wedlock vow;
Yea, the illiterate that know not how   *810*
   To cipher what is writ in learnèd books   811
   Will quote my loathsome trespass in my looks.   812

"The nurse to still her child will tell my story,
And fright her crying babe with Tarquin's name;
The orator to deck his oratory
Will couple my reproach to Tarquin's shame;
Feast-finding minstrels tuning my defame   817
   Will tie the hearers to attend each line,   818
   How Tarquin wrongèd me, I Collatine.

"Let my good name, that senseless reputation,   820
For Collatine's dear love be kept unspotted;
If that be made a theme for disputation,   822
The branches of another root are rotted,   823

---

800 *jealous* suspicious and inquisitive **803** *still* forever **805** *sepulchered* entombed **806** *object* object of scrutiny **807** *charactered* written **811** *cipher* spell, read **812** *quote* observe, take note of **817** *Feast-finding minstrels* singers who seek employment at banquets; *tuning my defame* singing of my disgrace **818** *tie* bind, captivate **820** *senseless* chaste, unsensual **822** *theme for disputation* topic of debate **823** *The . . . rotted* i.e., those of Collatine and his family as well as Lucrece's

And undeserved reproach to him allotted
825   That is as clear from this attaint of mine
As I ere this was pure to Collatine.

827 "O unseen shame, invisible disgrace!
828 O unfelt sore, crest-wounding private scar!
Reproach is stamped in Collatinus' face,
830 And Tarquin's eye may read the mot afar,
How he in peace is wounded, not in war.
        Alas, how many bear such shameful blows,
        Which not themselves but he that gives them knows!

"If, Collatine, thine honor lay in me,
From me by strong assault it is bereft:
My honey lost, and I, a dronelike bee,
837 Have no perfection of my summer left,
But robbed and ransacked by injurious theft.
        In thy weak hive a wandering wasp hath crept,
840   And sucked the honey which thy chaste bee kept.

841 "Yet am I guilty of thy honor's wrack;
Yet for thy honor did I entertain him;
843 Coming from thee, I could not put him back,
844 For it had been dishonor to disdain him;
Besides, of weariness he did complain him,
846   And talked of virtue: O unlooked-for evil,
        When virtue is profaned in such a devil!

848 "Why should the worm intrude the maiden bud,
Or hateful cuckoos hatch in sparrows' nests?
850 Or toads infect fair founts with venom mud?

---

825 *attaint* both "taint" and "accusation"   **827–28** *O unseen . . . scar* i.e.,
Collatine has suffered injury without yet knowing it   **828** *crest-wounding*
damaging to the family honor (crest)   **830** *mot* heraldic motto   **837** *perfec-
tion* excellence, abundance (of honey)   **841** *wrack* wreck   **843** *put him back*
refuse him admission   **844** *had* would have   **846** *unlooked-for* unexpected
848 *intrude* invade   **850** *founts* springs; *venom* toxic or polluting

Or tyrant folly lurk in gentle breasts?   851
Or kings be breakers of their own behests?   852
   But no perfection is so absolute
   That some impurity doth not pollute.

"The agèd man that coffers up his gold   855
Is plagued with cramps and gouts and painful fits,
And scarce hath eyes his treasure to behold;
But like still-pining Tantalus he sits,   858
And useless barns the harvest of his wits,   859
   Having no other pleasure of his gain   860
   But torment that it cannot cure his pain.

"So then he hath it when he cannot use it,   862
And leaves it to be mastered by his young,   863
Who in their pride do presently abuse it;
Their father was too weak and they too strong
To hold their cursèd-blessèd fortune long.
   The sweets we wish for turn to loathèd sours
   Even in the moment that we call them ours.

"Unruly blasts wait on the tender spring;   869
Unwholesome weeds take root with precious flowers;   870
The adder hisses where the sweet birds sing;
What virtue breeds iniquity devours.
We have no good that we can say is ours
   But ill-annexèd opportunity   874
   Or kills his life or else his quality.

"O opportunity, thy guilt is great!
'Tis thou that execut'st the traitor's treason;   877

---

851 *gentle* noble   852 *behests* laws   855 *coffers up* hoards in chests   858
still-pining ever-yearning; *Tantalus* mythical character condemned to eternal
hunger and thirst   859 *useless barns* uselessly hoards   862 *then* at that time
863 *mastered* controlled   869 *wait on* attend   874 *ill-annexèd* detrimentally
connected (i.e., chance circumstances can destroy life or corrupt intrinsic
virtue)   877 *execut'st* puts into effect

Thou sets the wolf where he the lamb may get;
879   Whoever plots the sin, thou point'st the season.
880   'Tis thou that spurn'st at right, at law, at reason;
    And in thy shady cell where none may spy him
    Sits sin, to seize the souls that wander by him.

883   "Thou mak'st the vestal violate her oath;
884   Thou blow'st the fire when temperance is thawed;
    Thou smother'st honesty, thou murd'rest troth,
886   Thou foul abettor, thou notorious bawd;
887   Thou plantest scandal, and displacest laud.
    Thou ravisher, thou traitor, thou false thief,
    Thy honey turns to gall, thy joy to grief.

890   "Thy secret pleasure turns to open shame,
    Thy private feasting to a public fast,
892   Thy smoothing titles to a ragged name,
    Thy sugared tongue to bitter wormwood taste;
894   Thy violent vanities can never last.
    How comes it then, vile opportunity,
    Being so bad, such numbers seek for thee?

897   "When wilt thou be the humble suppliant's friend,
    And bring him where his suit may be obtained?
899   When wilt thou sort an hour great strifes to end,
900   Or free that soul which wretchedness hath chained,
901   Give physic to the sick, ease to the pained?
    The poor, lame, blind, halt, creep, cry out for thee;
902   But they ne'er meet with opportunity.

---

879 *point'st* appoints   880 *spurn'st at* flouts   883 *vestal* (Roman) virgin religiously dedicated to chastity   884 *blow'st the fire* fan the flame of lust   886 *abettor* accomplice; *notorious bawd* infamous pimp   887 *plantest* propagate; *displacest laud* either "misdirect" or "replace" praise   892 *smoothing* flattering; *ragged* damaged   894 *vanities* futile, worldly delights   897 *suppliant* pleader   899 *sort* set aside   901 *physic* medicine   902 *halt* lame

"The patient dies while the physician sleeps;
The orphan pines while the oppressor feeds;   905
Justice is feasting while the widow weeps;
Advice is sporting while infection breeds.   907
Thou grant'st no time for charitable deeds;
    Wrath, envy, treason, rape, and murder's rages,
     Thy heinous hours wait on them as their pages.   910

"When truth and virtue have to do with thee,
A thousand crosses keep them from thy aid;   912
They buy thy help, but sin ne'er gives a fee: 913
He gratis comes, and thou art well appaid   914
As well to hear as grant what he hath said.
    My Collatine would else have come to me
     When Tarquin did, but he was stayed by thee.   917

"Guilty thou art of murder and of theft,
Guilty of perjury and subornation,   919
Guilty of treason, forgery, and shift,   920
Guilty of incest, that abomination:
An accessary by thine inclination
    To all sins past and all that are to come
     From the creation to the general doom.

"Misshapen time, copesmate of ugly night,   925
Swift subtle post, carrier of grisly care,   926
Eater of youth, false slave to false delight,
Base watch of woes, sin's packhorse, virtue's snare;   928
Thou nursest all, and murderest all that are.
    O hear me then, injurious shifting Time;   930
     Be guilty of my death, since of my crime.

---

905 *pines* starves   907 *Advice* medical aid   910 *heinous* wicked   912 *crosses* obstacles   913 *They . . . fee* i.e., they must pay for the help sin gets free   914 *appaid* content   917 *stayed* detained   919 *subornation* inducement to commit perjury   920 *shift* trickery   925 *copesmate* accomplice   926 *post* messenger; *carrier* bearer, conveyor   928 *watch* watchman; *packhorse* horse that carries goods   930 *shifting* changing, deceiving

"Why hath thy servant opportunity
Betrayed the hours thou gav'st me to repose,
934 Canceled my fortunes and enchainèd me
935 To endless date of never-ending woes?
936 Time's office is to fine the hate of foes,
     To eat up errors by opinion bred,
938   Not spend the dowry of a lawful bed.

"Time's glory is to calm contending kings,
940 To unmask falsehood and bring truth to light,
941 To stamp the seal of time in agèd things,
942 To wake the morn and sentinel the night,
     To wrong the wronger till he render right,
944   To ruinate proud buildings with thy hours,
       And smear with dust their glittering golden towers;

946 "To fill with wormholes stately monuments,
947 To feed oblivion with decay of things,
948 To blot old books and alter their contents,
949 To pluck the quills from ancient ravens' wings,
950 To dry the old oak's sap and cherish springs,
     To spoil antiquities of hammered steel,
952   And turn the giddy round of fortune's wheel;

953 "To show the beldame daughters of her daughter,
     To make the child a man, the man a child,
     To slay the tiger that doth live by slaughter,
     To tame the unicorn and lion wild,

---

934 *Canceled my fortunes* undone my good fortune   935 *endless date* i.e., a
bond of misery without a terminal date   936 *office* duty, function; *fine* end,
punish   938 *spend . . . bed* expend (waste) the treasure of marriage   941 *To
stamp . . . things* to place its stamp of approval on what has endured   942
sentinel keep watch over   944 *ruinate* reduce to ruin   946 *stately monuments*
proud relics of the past   947 *feed oblivion* consign to forgetfulness   948 *blot*
smudge; *alter their contents* change their meanings   949 *ravens* (proverbially
long-lived birds)   950 *cherish springs* foster new growth   952 *Fortune's
wheel* wheel, turned by the goddess Fortune, by which the ups and downs of
life are determined   953 *beldame* old woman

To mock the subtle in themselves beguiled,   957
  To cheer the plowman with increaseful crops,   958
  And waste huge stones with little water drops.   959

"Why work'st thou mischief in thy pilgrimage,   960
Unless thou couldst return to make amends?
One poor retiring minute in an age   962
Would purchase thee a thousand thousand friends,
Lending him wit that to bad debtors lends.   964
  O this dread night, wouldst thou one hour come back,
  I could prevent this storm and shun thy wrack!   966

"Thou ceaseless lackey to eternity,   967
With some mischance cross Tarquin in his flight;   968
Devise extremes beyond extremity,
To make him curse this cursèd crimeful night.   970
Let ghastly shadows his lewd eyes affright,
  And the dire thought of his committed evil
  Shape every bush a hideous shapeless devil.

"Disturb his hours of rest with restless trances;   974
Afflict him in his bed with bedrid groans;   975
Let there bechance him pitiful mischances,   976
To make him moan, but pity not his moans.
Stone him with hardened hearts harder than stones,
  And let mild women to him lose their mildness,
  Wilder to him than tigers in their wildness.   980

"Let him have time to tear his curlèd hair,
Let him have time against himself to rave,
Let him have time of time's help to despair,
Let him have time to live a loathèd slave,

---

957 *the subtle . . . beguiled* the clever cheats who outsmart themselves 958
increaseful profitable, burgeoning 959 *waste* wear away 960 *pilgrimage*
i.e., onward course of time 962 *poor retiring minute* i.e., mere moment of
return 964 *wit* foreknowledge, intelligence 966 *prevent* forestall; *shun thy
wrack* avoid the ruin you have brought about 967 *lackey* servant 968 *cross*
hinder 974 *trances* semiconscious states 975 *bedrid* bedridden 976
bechance chance to happen

985 Let him have time a beggar's orts to crave,
    And time to see one that by alms doth live
    Disdain to him disdainèd scraps to give.

"Let him have time to see his friends his foes,
And merry fools to mock at him resort;
990 Let him have time to mark how slow time goes
In time of sorrow, and how swift and short
His time of folly and his time of sport;
993   And ever let his unrecalling crime
    Have time to wail the abusing of his time.

"O time, thou tutor both to good and bad,
Teach me to curse him that thou taught'st this ill;
At his own shadow let the thief run mad,
Himself himself seek every hour to kill;
Such wretched hands such wretched blood should spill;
1000   For who so base would such an office have
1001   As slanderous deathsman to so base a slave?

1002 "The baser is he, coming from a king,
To shame his hope with deeds degenerate;
The mightier man, the mightier is the thing
That makes him honored or begets him hate;
For greatest scandal waits on greatest state.
1007   The moon being clouded presently is missed,
    But little stars may hide them when they list.

"The crow may bathe his coal-black wings in mire,
1010 And unperceived fly with the filth away;
But if the like the snow-white swan desire,
The stain upon his silver down will stay.

---

985 orts scraps   **993** *unrecalling* irrevocable   **1001** *slanderous deathsman* ex-
ecutioner, rendered infamous by his trade   **1002** *coming* descended
1007–08 *The moon . . . list* i.e., when the moon is clouded over, its absence
is noticed at once, but the disappearance of small stars is unnoticed, there-
fore unimportant; they can "hide" at will

Poor grooms are sightless night, kings glorious day;   1013
   Gnats are unnoted wheresoe'er they fly,
   But eagles gazed upon with every eye.

"Out, idle words, servants to shallow fools,   1016
Unprofitable sounds, weak arbitrators!   1017
Busy yourselves in skill-contending schools;   1018
Debate where leisure serves with dull debaters;   1019
To trembling clients be you mediators: 1020
   For me, I force not argument a straw,   1021
   Since that my case is past the help of law.

"In vain I rail at opportunity,
At time, at Tarquin, and uncheerful night;
In vain I cavil with mine infamy,   1025
In vain I spurn at my confirmed despite;   1026
This helpless smoke of words doth me no right: 1027
   The remedy indeed to do me good
   Is to let forth my foul defilèd blood.

"Poor hand, why quiver'st thou at this decree?   1030
Honor thyself to rid me of this shame;
For if I die, my honor lives in thee,
But if I live, thou liv'st in my defame.   1033
Since thou couldst not defend thy loyal dame,   1034
   And wast afeard to scratch her wicked foe,
   Kill both thyself and her for yielding so."

This said, from her betumbled couch she starteth,   1037
To find some desperate instrument of death;
But this no slaughterhouse no tool imparteth   1039

1013 *sightless* invisible, unnoticed 1016 *Out* away with 1017 *arbitrators* judges of cases in dispute 1018 *skill-contending schools* academic institutions in which rhetoric is taught 1019 *dull* i.e., long-winded 1021 *force . . . a straw* don't give a straw for arguments 1025 *cavil with* frivolously dispute 1026 *despite* shame 1027 *helpless* unavailing 1033 *defame* infamy 1034 *dame* mistress 1037 *betumbled* disordered 1039 *imparteth* supplies

1040 To make more vent for passage of her breath,
Which thronging through her lips so vanisheth
1042   As smoke from Etna that in air consumes,
Or that which from dischargèd cannon fumes.

"In vain," quoth she, "I live, and seek in vain
Some happy mean to end a hapless life.
1046 I feared by Tarquin's falchion to be slain,
Yet for the selfsame purpose seek a knife;
But when I feared, I was a loyal wife:
So am I now – O no, that cannot be;
1050   Of that true type hath Tarquin rifled me.

"O, that is gone for which I sought to live,
And therefore now I need not fear to die.
1053 To clear this spot by death, at least I give
A badge of fame to slander's livery,
1055 A dying life to living infamy.
1056   Poor helpless help, the treasure stolen away,
To burn the guiltless casket where it lay!

"Well, well, dear Collatine, thou shalt not know
The stainèd taste of violated troth;
1060 I will not wrong thy true affection so
To flatter thee with an infringèd oath;
1062 This bastard graff shall never come to growth:
1063   He shall not boast who did thy stock pollute
That thou art doting father of his fruit.

"Nor shall he smile at thee in secret thought,
Nor laugh with his companions at thy state;

1042 *consumes* vanishes   1046 *falchion* sword   1050 *type* character type; *ri-fled* robbed   1053 *spot* blemish   1053–54 *I give . . . livery* i.e., I attach one token of honor to the raiment of ill-repute   1055 *A dying . . . infamy* i.e., a death to living shame   1056 *helpless* unhelpful   1062 *bastard graff* slip grafted on to a plant stem (here implying possible impregnation)   1063 *stock* breeding material

But thou shalt know thy interest was not bought   1067
Basely with gold, but stolen from forth thy gate.
For me, I am the mistress of my fate,
 And with my trespass never will dispense,   1070
 Till life to death acquit my forced offense.   1071

"I will not poison thee with my attaint,   1072
Nor fold my fault in cleanly coined excuses;   1073
My sable ground of sin I will not paint   1074
To hide the truth of this false night's abuses.
My tongue shall utter all; mine eyes, like sluices,   1076
 As from a mountain spring that feeds a dale,
 Shall gush pure streams to purge my impure tale."

By this, lamenting Philomel had ended   1079
The well-tuned warble of her nightly sorrow,   1080
And solemn night with slow sad gait descended
To ugly hell; when lo, the blushing morrow
Lends light to all fair eyes that light will borrow;
 But cloudy Lucrece shames herself to see,
 And therefore still in night would cloistered be.   1085

Revealing day through every cranny spies,
And seems to point her out where she sits weeping;
To whom she sobbing speaks: "O eye of eyes,
Why pry'st thou through my window? Leave thy peeping;

1067 *interest* property, investment   1070 *dispense* (give) pardon   1071 *acquit* exonerate, cancel   1072 *attaint* crime, infection   1073 *cleanly coined* newly minted, well counterfeited   1074 *sable ground* dark underlying hue   1076 *sluices* conduits   1079 *Philomel* (in Ovid's *Metamorphoses*, a woman raped by her brother-in-law Tereus, who also cuts out her tongue to silence her; the gods eventually turn Philomel into a nightingale, a melancholy nocturnal singer; cf. Shakespeare's *Titus Andronicus*)   1080 *warble* song   1085 *cloistered* sheltered

1090 Mock with thy tickling beams eyes that are sleeping;
    Brand not my forehead with thy piercing light,
    For day hath naught to do what's done by night."

1093 Thus cavils she with everything she sees.
1094 True grief is fond and testy as a child,
1095 Who wayward once, his mood with naught agrees;
1096 Old woes, not infant sorrows, bear them mild.
1097 Continuance tames the one; the other wild,
    Like an unpracticed swimmer plunging still,
    With too much labor drowns for want of skill.

1100 So she deep drenchèd in a sea of care
1101 Holds disputation with each thing she views,
    And to herself all sorrow doth compare;
    No object but her passion's strength renews,
1104 And as one shifts, another straight ensues.
    Sometime her grief is dumb and hath no words,
    Sometime 'tis mad and too much talk affords.

    The little birds that tune their morning's joy
    Make her moans mad with their sweet melody;
1109 For mirth doth search the bottom of annoy;
1110 Sad souls are slain in merry company;
    Grief best is pleased with grief's society.
1112   True sorrow then is feelingly sufficed
1113   When with like semblance it is sympathized.

1114 'Tis double death to drown in ken of shore;
1115 He ten times pines that pines beholding food;

1090 *tickling* sexually intrusive, sensually arousing   1093 *cavils* quibbles
1094 *fond* foolish; *testy* irritable   1095 *wayward* difficult   1096 *bear them*
conduct themselves   1097 *Continuance* having become accustomed   1101
disputation debate   1104 *ensues* replaces it   1109 *search the bottom* sound
the depths; *annoy* distress   1112 *feelingly sufficed* (has) its feelings satisfied
1113 *is sympathized* is matched in feeling by   1114 *ken* sight   1115 *pines*
starves

To see the salve doth make the wound ache more;   1116
Great grief grieves most at that would do it good;   1117
Deep woes roll forward like a gentle flood,
   Who, being stopped, the bounding banks o'erflows;   1119
   Grief dallied with nor law nor limit knows.   1120

"You mocking birds," quoth she, "your tunes entomb
Within your hollow-swelling feathered breasts,
And in my hearing be you mute and dumb;
My restless discord loves no stops nor rests;   1124
A woeful hostess brooks not merry guests.   1125
   Relish your nimble notes to pleasing ears;   1126
   Distress likes dumps, when time is kept with tears.   1127

"Come, Philomel, that sing'st of ravishment,
Make thy sad grove in my disheveled hair.
As the dank earth weeps at thy languishment,   1130
So I at each sad strain will strain a tear,   1131
And with deep groans the diapason bear;   1132
   For burden-wise I'll hum on Tarquin still,   1133
   While thou on Tereus descants better skill.   1134

"And whiles against a thorn thou bear'st thy part   1135
To keep thy sharp woes waking, wretched I,   1136
To imitate thee well, against my heart
Will fix a sharp knife to affright mine eye,

1116 *salve* medicine, ointment   1117 *grieves* is offended by   1119 *stopped*
obstructed   1120 *dallied with* frivolously obstructed   1124 *stops nor rests*
pauses, interruptions   1125 *brooks* endures   1126 *Relish* sing   1127 *dumps*
sad music, gloominess   1130 *languishment* sorrow   1131 *strain a tear* distill
a tear   1132 *diapason* harmonious accompaniment   1133 *burden-wise* in
accompaniment   1134 *descants* sing in a high voice   1135–36 *And . . .
waking* (Philomel pressed her breast against a thorn to keep awake at night
and be reminded of her pain)

Who if it wink shall thereon fall and die:
1140   These means as frets upon an instrument
1141   Shall tune our heartstrings to true languishment.

"And for, poor bird, thou sing'st not in the day,
As shaming any eye should thee behold,
1144 Some dark deep desert seated from the way,
That knows not parching heat nor freezing cold,
Will we find out; and there we will unfold
1147   To creatures stern sad tunes to change their kinds:
Since men prove beasts, let beasts bear gentle minds."

1149 As the poor frighted deer that stands at gaze,
1150 Wildly determining which way to fly,
1151 Or one encompassed with a winding maze,
That cannot tread the way out readily,
1153 So with herself is she in mutiny,
To live or die which of the twain were better
1155   When life is shamed and death reproach's debtor.

"To kill myself," quoth she, "alack, what were it,
1157 But with my body my poor soul's pollution?
They that lose half with greater patience bear it
Than they whose whole is swallowed in confusion.
1160 That mother tries a merciless conclusion
Who, having two sweet babes, when death takes one,
Will slay the other and be nurse to none.

"My body or my soul, which was the dearer,
When the one pure the other made divine?

1140 *frets* ridges on the fingerboard of a stringed instrument; irritations
1141 *languishment* i.e., melancholy   1144 *seated from the way* placed out of
the way   1147 *kinds* natures (alludes to the power of Orpheus's song to tame
wild beasts)   1149 *at gaze* immobilized and glancing wildly   1151 *encompassed with* lost within, enclosed by   1153 *in mutiny* in conflict or revolt
1155 *death . . . debtor* death (by suicide) would incur blame   1157 *But . . .
pollution* i.e., to add pollution of my soul to my bodily pollution   1160 *conclusion* experiment

Whose love of either to myself was nearer,
When both were kept for heaven and Collatine?
Ay me, the bark pilled from the lofty pine,   1167
  His leaves will wither and his sap decay;
  So must my soul, her bark being pilled away.

"Her house is sacked, her quiet interrupted,   1170
Her mansion battered by the enemy,
Her sacred temple spotted, spoiled, corrupted,   1172
Grossly engirt with daring infamy.   1173
Then let it not be called impiety
  If in this blemished fort I make some hole
  Through which I may convey this troubled soul.

"Yet die I will not till my Collatine
Have heard the cause of my untimely death,
That he may vow in that sad hour of mine
Revenge on him that made me stop my breath.   *1180*
My stainèd blood to Tarquin I'll bequeath,
  Which by him tainted shall for him be spent,   1182
  And as his due writ in my testament.   1183

"My honor I'll bequeath unto the knife
That wounds my body so dishonorèd.
'Tis honor to deprive dishonored life;
The one will live, the other being dead.
So of shame's ashes shall my fame be bred;   1188
  For in my death I murder shameful scorn:
  My shame so dead, mine honor is new born.   *1190*

"Dear lord of that dear jewel I have lost,   1191
What legacy shall I bequeath to thee?
My resolution, love, shall be thy boast,

1167 *pilled* peeled 1170 *house* i.e., the body, "house" of the soul; *sacked* pillaged 1172 *spotted* besmirched 1173 *Grossly engirt* coarsely or indecently encircled 1182 *spent* shed, expended 1183 *writ . . . testament* left in my will 1188–90 *So . . . born* i.e., like the phoenix, her good reputation will be reborn from the ashes of her life 1191 *jewel* her honor

By whose example thou revenged mayst be.
How Tarquin must be used, read it in me:
    Myself thy friend will kill myself thy foe;
    And for my sake serve thou false Tarquin so.

1198 "This brief abridgment of my will I make:
My soul and body to the skies and ground;
1200 My resolution, husband, do thou take;
Mine honor be the knife's that makes my wound;
My shame be his that did my fame confound;
1203   And all my fame that lives disbursèd be
    To those that live and think no shame of me.

"Thou, Collatine, shalt oversee this will;
1206 How was I overseen that thou shalt see it!
1207 My blood shall wash the slander of mine ill;
My life's foul deed, my life's fair end shall free it.
Faint not, faint heart, but stoutly say 'So be it';
1210   Yield to my hand, my hand shall conquer thee:
    Thou dead, both die, and both shall victors be."

This plot of death when sadly she had laid,
1213 And wiped the brinish pearl from her bright eyes,
1214 With untuned tongue she hoarsely calls her maid,
Whose swift obedience to her mistress hies;
1216 For fleet-winged duty with thought's feathers flies.
    Poor Lucrece' cheeks unto her maid seem so
1218   As winter meads when sun doth melt their snow.

Her mistress she doth give demure good morrow
1220 With soft slow tongue, true mark of modesty,
1221 And sorts a sad look to her lady's sorrow,
1222 For why her face wore sorrow's livery;

1198 *abridgment* précis, summary   1203 *disbursèd* paid out   1206 *How . . .
see it* how I was so badly cheated that you shall see it   1207 *slander* infamy
1213 *brinish pearl* i.e., salty, glistening tears   1214 *untuned* harsh-sounding
1216 *with . . . flies* moves as quickly as thought   1218 *meads* meadows
1221 *sorts* adapts   1222 *For why* because; *livery* servant's uniform

But durst not ask of her audaciously
   Why her two suns were cloud-eclipsèd so,   1224
   Nor why her fair cheeks over-washed with woe.

But as the earth doth weep, the sun being set,
Each flower moistened like a melting eye,
Even so the maid with swelling drops 'gan wet
Her circled eyne, enforced by sympathy   1229
Of those fair suns set in her mistress' sky,   1230
   Who in a salt-waved ocean quench their light,
   Which makes the maid weep like the dewy night.

A pretty while these pretty creatures stand,   1233
Like ivory conduits coral cisterns filling.   1234
One justly weeps; the other takes in hand   1235
No cause but company of her drops' spilling.
Their gentle sex to weep are often willing,
   Grieving themselves to guess at others' smarts,   1238
   And then they drown their eyes or break their hearts.

For men have marble, women waxen, minds,   1240
And therefore are they formed as marble will;   1241
The weak oppressed, the impression of strange kinds   1242
Is formed in them by force, by fraud, or skill.
Then call them not the authors of their ill,   1244
   No more than wax shall be accounted evil
   Wherein is stamped the semblance of a devil.

Their smoothness, like a goodly champaign plain,   1247
Lays open all the little worms that creep;   1248
In men, as in a rough-grown grove, remain

1224 *suns* eyes   1229 *eyne* eyes   1229–32 *enforced . . . night* i.e., the maid
weeps in sympathy with the mistress, whose eyes are drowned in tears   1233
A pretty while a little while   1234 *conduits* pipes   1235 *justly* with good rea-
son; *takes in hand* undertakes   1238 *smarts* pains   1241 *as marble will* as
the stone (marble) determines   1242 *the impression . . . kinds* the imprint of
things foreign (to them) by nature   1244 *authors* doers   1247 *champaign*
plain flat, open ground   1248 *Lays open* exposes

1250 Cave-keeping evils that obscurely sleep;
1251 Through crystal walls each little mote will peep.
　　　Though men can cover crimes with bold stern looks,
　　　Poor women's faces are their own faults' books.

1254 No man inveigh against the withered flower,
　　　But chide rough winter that the flower hath killed;
1256 Not that devoured, but that which doth devour,
1257 Is worthy blame. O, let it not be hild
1258 Poor women's faults that they are so fulfilled
1259 　　With men's abuses: those proud lords to blame
1260 　　Make weak-made women tenants to their shame.

1261 The precedent whereof in Lucrece view,
1262 Assailed by night with circumstances strong
　　　Of present death, and shame that might ensue
　　　By that her death, to do her husband wrong;
1265 Such danger to resistance did belong
1266 　　That dying fear through all her body spread;
　　　And who cannot abuse a body dead?

1268 By this, mild patience bid fair Lucrece speak
1269 To the poor counterfeit of her complaining.
1270 "My girl," quoth she, "on what occasion break
　　　Those tears from thee that down thy cheeks are raining?
1272 If thou dost weep for grief of my sustaining,
　　　Know, gentle wench, it small avails my mood:
　　　If tears could help, mine own would do me good.

1250 *Cave-keeping* i.e., hidden; *obscurely sleep* lie dormant　1251 *mote* speck
1254 *inveigh* utter complaints　1256 *Not that* not that which　1257 *hild*
held　1258 *fulfilled* filled full　1259 *to blame* blameworthy　1260
tenants . . . shame i.e., men "own" the shame that women inhabit as "tenants"
1261 *precedent* prototype, example　1262 *circumstances strong* strong indica-
tions　1265 *Such danger . . . belong* resistance would necessarily have been so
dangerous　1266 *dying fear* fear of death, paralyzing fear　1268 *By this* by
this time　1269 *poor counterfeit* pale imitation　1272 *of my sustaining* which
I sustain

"But tell me, girl, when went" – and there she stayed,
Till after a deep groan – "Tarquin from hence?"
"Madam, ere I was up," replied the maid,
"The more to blame my sluggard negligence.   1278
Yet with the fault I thus far can dispense: 1279
   Myself was stirring ere the break of day,   *1280*
   And ere I rose was Tarquin gone away.

"But lady, if your maid may be so bold,
She would request to know your heaviness."
"O, peace," quoth Lucrece, "if it should be told,
The repetition cannot make it less;
For more it is than I can well express,
   And that deep torture may be called a hell,
   When more is felt than one hath power to tell.

"Go, get me hither paper, ink, and pen;
Yet save that labor, for I have them here.   *1290*
What should I say? One of my husband's men
Bid thou be ready by and by to bear
A letter to my lord, my love, my dear.
   Bid him with speed prepare to carry it;
   The cause craves haste, and it will soon be writ."

Her maid is gone, and she prepares to write,
First hovering o'er the paper with her quill;
Conceit and grief an eager combat fight;   1298
What wit sets down is blotted straight with will;   1299
This is too curious good, this blunt and ill.   1300
   Much like a press of people at a door
   Throng her inventions, which shall go before.   1302

At last she thus begins: "Thou worthy lord
Of that unworthy wife that greeteth thee,

1278 *sluggard* slothful   1279 *dispense* excuse   1298 *Conceit* thought, style
1299 *What . . . will* what thought expresses is marred by passion   1300
curious good ornate; *blunt* clumsy   1302 *inventions* ideas, topics

1305 Health to thy person! Next, vouchsafe t' afford –
     If ever, love, thy Lucrece thou wilt see –
     Some present speed to come and visit me.
         So I commend me, from our house in grief;
         My woes are tedious, though my words are brief."

1310 Here folds she up the tenor of her woe,
     Her certain sorrow writ uncertainly.
1312 By this short schedule Collatine may know
     Her grief, but not her grief's true quality;
1314 She dares not thereof make discovery,
1315   Lest he should hold it her own gross abuse,
1316   Ere she with blood had stained her stained excuse.

     Besides, the life and feeling of her passion
     She hoards, to spend when he is by to hear her,
1319 When sighs and groans and tears may grace the fashion
1320 Of her disgrace, the better so to clear her
     From that suspicion which the world might bear her.
1322   To shun this blot, she would not blot the letter
         With words, till action might become them better.

     To see sad sights moves more than hear them told,
     For then the eye interprets to the ear
1326 The heavy motion that it doth behold,
     When every part a part of woe doth bear.
     'Tis but a part of sorrow that we hear;
         Deep sounds make lesser noise than shallow fords,
1330   And sorrow ebbs, being blown with wind of words.

     Her letter now is sealed, and on it writ
     "At Ardea to my lord with more than haste."

1305 *vouchsafe t' afford* deign to grant   1310 *tenor* message, tune   1312
schedule inventory   1314 *make discovery* reveal   1315 *gross abuse* grave mis-
conduct   1316 *Ere . . . excuse* before she had expunged her guilty excuse
with her own blood   1319 *grace the fashion* enhance the presentation   1322
To shun . . . letter i.e., to avoid suspicion, she would not write   1326 *heavy
motion* sad feeling or action

The post attends, and she delivers it,   1333
Charging the sour-faced groom to hie as fast
As lagging fowls before the northern blast.
   Speed more than speed but dull and slow she deems:
   Extremity still urgeth such extremes.

The homely villain curtsies to her low,   1338
And blushing on her, with a steadfast eye
Receives the scroll without or yea or no,   *1340*
And forth with bashful innocence doth hie.
But they whose guilt within their bosoms lie
   Imagine every eye beholds their blame;
   For Lucrece thought he blushed to see her shame:

When, silly groom, God wot, it was defect   1345
Of spirit, life, and bold audacity;
Such harmless creatures have a true respect   1347
To talk in deeds, while others saucily
Promise more speed, but do it leisurely.
   Even so this pattern of the worn-out age   1350
   Pawned honest looks, but laid no words to gage.   1351

His kindled duty kindled her mistrust,   1352
That two red fires in both their faces blazed;
She thought he blushed as knowing Tarquin's lust,
And blushing with him, wistly on him gazed.   1355
Her earnest eye did make him more amazed;
   The more she saw the blood his cheeks replenish,
   The more she thought he spied in her some blemish.

But long she thinks till he return again,
And yet the duteous vassal scarce is gone.   1360
The weary time she cannot entertain,   1361

1333 *post* messenger 1338 *homely villain* common servingman; *curtsies*
bows 1345 *silly* simple; *wot* knows 1347 *respect* intent 1350 *pattern . . .
age* model of an earlier and better time 1351 *Pawned* pledged (i.e., honest
looks rather than words) 1352 *kindled duty* aroused desire to serve 1355
wistly intently 1360 *vassal* servant 1361 *entertain* occupy

For now 'tis stale to sigh, to weep, and groan;
So woe hath wearied woe, moan tirèd moan,
    That she her plaints a little while doth stay,
    Pausing for means to mourn some newer way.

At last she calls to mind where hangs a piece
1367 Of skillful painting made for Priam's Troy,
Before the which is drawn the power of Greece,
1369 For Helen's rape the city to destroy,
1370 Threatening cloud-kissing Ilion with annoy;
1371   Which the conceited painter drew so proud
    As heaven, it seemed, to kiss the turrets bowed.

A thousand lamentable objects there
In scorn of nature art gave lifeless life;
Many a dry drop seemed a weeping tear,
Shed for the slaughtered husband by the wife;
1377 The red blood reeked to show the painter's strife,
    And dying eyes gleamed forth their ashy lights
    Like dying coals burnt out in tedious nights.

1380 There might you see the laboring pioneer
Begrimed with sweat and smearèd all with dust;
And from the towers of Troy there would appear
The very eyes of men through loopholes thrust,
Gazing upon the Greeks with little lust.
1385   Such sweet observance in this work was had
    That one might see those far-off eyes look sad.

1367 *for* of; *Priam's Troy* (the city of Troy, ruled by King Priam and besieged by Greek forces, in Homer's epic poem *The Iliad*) **1369** *Helen's rape* (the seizure of the Greek Helen by the Trojan Paris was the cause of the Trojan War; "rape" alludes here to forcible abduction) **1370** *Ilion* (poetic name for Troy); *annoy* harm **1371** *conceited* ingenious **1377** *reeked* smoked **1380** *pioneer* i.e., one who digs trenches or undermines opposing defenses **1385** *sweet observance* pleasing attention to detail

In great commanders, grace and majesty
You might behold, triumphing in their faces;   1388
In youth, quick bearing and dexterity;   1389
And here and there the painter interlaces   1390
Pale cowards marching on with trembling paces,
 Which heartless peasants did so well resemble   1392
 That one would swear he saw them quake and tremble.

In Ajax and Ulysses, O what art   1394
Of physiognomy might one behold!   1395
The face of either ciphered either's heart;   1396
Their face their manners most expressly told:
In Ajax' eyes blunt rage and rigor rolled,   1398
 But the mild glance that sly Ulysses lent
 Showed deep regard and smiling government.   1400

There pleading might you see grave Nestor stand,   1401
As 'twere encouraging the Greeks to fight,
Making such sober action with his hand   1403
That it beguiled attention, charmed the sight;   1404
In speech it seemed his beard all silver white
 Wagged up and down, and from his lips did fly
 Thin winding breath which purled up to the sky.   1407

About him were a press of gaping faces
Which seemed to swallow up his sound advice;
All jointly listening, but with several graces,   1410
As if some mermaid did their ears entice;

1388 *triumphing* showing forth gloriously   1389 *quick* lively   1390 *inter-laces* interweaves   1392 *heartless* lacking courage   1394 *Ajax, Ulysses* heroes of the Greeks   1395 *physiognomy* representations of character through appearance   1396 *either* each; *ciphered* expressed, as if in writing   1398 *rigor* sternness, cruelty   1400 *regard* respect, thoughtfulness; *smiling government* easy control of himself and others   1401 *Nestor* aged Greek counselor   1403 *sober* restrained   1404 *beguiled* solicited; *charmed* attracted and pleased   1407 *purled* curled   1410 *several graces* differing attitudes

1412 Some high, some low, the painter was so nice.
    The scalps of many almost hid behind
1414   To jump up higher seemed, to mock the mind.

    Here one man's hand leaned on another's head,
    His nose being shadowed by his neighbor's ear;
1417 Here one being thronged bears back, all boll'n and red;
1418 Another smothered seems to pelt and swear;
    And in their rage such signs of rage they bear
1420   As, but for loss of Nestor's golden words,
    It seemed they would debate with angry swords.

1422 For much imaginary work was there;
1423 Conceit deceitful, so compact, so kind,
    That for Achilles' image stood his spear
    Gripped in an armèd hand; himself behind
    Was left unseen, save to the eye of mind:
    A hand, a foot, a face, a leg, a head,
    Stood for the whole to be imaginèd.

1429 And from the walls of strong-besiegèd Troy,
1430 When their brave hope, bold Hector, marched to field,
    Stood many Trojan mothers sharing joy
    To see their youthful sons bright weapons wield;
1433 And to their hope they such odd action yield
    That through their light joy seemèd to appear,
    Like bright things stained, a kind of heavy fear.

1436 And from the strand of Dardan where they fought
1437 To Simois' reedy banks the red blood ran,

1412 *high . . . low* tall, short; *nice* precise   1414 *mock* tease and astonish
1417 *thronged* crowded; *boll'n* swollen (with anger)   1418 *smothered*
crushed; *pelt* cry out angrily   1420 *but for loss of* except that they feared to
lose   1422 *imaginary work* work of, and appealing to, the imagination
1423 *Conceit deceitful* deceiving (artistic) conception; *compact* substantial,
well crafted; *kind* natural   1429 *strong-besiegèd* beleaguered   1433 *such . . .
yield* give such contradictory expression   1436 *strand* shore; *Dardan* (region
in which Troy was located)   1437 *Simois* (river close to Troy)

Whose waves to imitate the battle sought
With swelling ridges, and their ranks began   1439
To break upon the gallèd shore, and then   1440
   Retire again, till meeting greater ranks
   They join, and shoot their foam at Simois' banks.

To this well-painted piece is Lucrece come,
To find a face where all distress is stelled.   1444
Many she sees where cares have carvèd some,
But none where all distress and dolor dwelled,   1446
Till she despairing Hecuba beheld,   1447
   Staring on Priam's wounds with her old eyes,
   Which bleeding under Pyrrhus' proud foot lies.   1449

In her the painter had anatomized   1450
Time's ruin, beauty's wrack, and grim care's reign;   1451
Her cheeks with chops and wrinkles were disguised;   1452
Of what she was no semblance did remain.
Her blue blood changed to black in every vein,   1454
   Wanting the spring that those shrunk pipes had fed,   1455
   Showed life imprisoned in a body dead.

On this sad shadow Lucrece spends her eyes,   1457
And shapes her sorrow to the beldame's woes,   1458
Who nothing wants to answer her but cries   1459
And bitter words to ban her cruel foes;   1460
The painter was no god to lend her those;
   And therefore Lucrece swears he did her wrong,
   To give her so much grief, and not a tongue.

1439 *ridges* crests   1440 *gallèd* eroded   1444 *stelled* portrayed   1446 *dolor*
misery   1447 *Hecuba* wife of Priam and queen of Troy   1449 *Which* who;
Pyrrhus ruthless Greek warrior who kills Priam (for an extended description,
see *Hamlet*, II.2)   1450 *anatomized* dissected   1451 *wrack* wreckage   1452
chops cracks   1454 *blue* i.e., living   1455 *Wanting* lacking   1457 *shadow*
both "remnant" and "image"   1458 *beldame* ancient woman   1459 *wants*
lacks   1460 *ban* curse

"Poor instrument," quoth she, "without a sound,
1465 I'll tune thy woes with my lamenting tongue,
1466 And drop sweet balm in Priam's painted wound,
And rail on Pyrrhus that hath done him wrong,
And with my tears quench Troy that burns so long;
    And with my knife scratch out the angry eyes
1470   Of all the Greeks that are thine enemies.

1471 "Show me the strumpet that began this stir,
That with my nails her beauty I may tear.
1473 Thy heat of lust, fond Paris, did incur
This load of wrath that burning Troy doth bear;
Thy eye kindled the fire that burneth here;
    And here in Troy, for trespass of thine eye,
1477   The sire, the son, the dame and daughter die.

"Why should the private pleasure of someone
1479 Become the public plague of many moe?
1480 Let sin alone committed light alone
Upon his head that hath transgressèd so;
Let guiltless souls be freed from guilty woe:
    For one's offense why should so many fall,
1484   To plague a private sin in general?

"Lo, here weeps Hecuba, here Priam dies,
1486 Here manly Hector faints, here Troilus swounds,
1487 Here friend by friend in bloody channel lies,
1488 And friend to friend gives unadvisèd wounds,
And one man's lust these many lives confounds.
1490   Had doting Priam checked his son's desire,
    Troy had been bright with fame, and not with fire."

1465 *tune* give voice   1466 *balm* healing ointment   1471 *strumpet* whore
(i.e., Helen)   1473 *fond* doting, foolish; *incur* bring down   1477 *sire* father
1479 *moe* more   1480 *light* descend   1484 *plague* punish   1486 *Troilus*
another Trojan hero, one of the royal princes (cf. Shakespeare's *Troilus and
Cressida*); *swounds* faints   1487 *channel* gutter   1488 *unadvisèd* unintended
1490 *doting* infatuated, senile

Here feelingly she weeps Troy's painted woes;
For sorrow, like a heavy hanging bell
Once set on ringing, with his own weight goes;   1494
Then little strength rings out the doleful knell.
So Lucrece, set a-work, sad tales doth tell
    To penciled pensiveness and colored sorrow: 1497
    She lends them words, and she their looks doth borrow.

She throws her eyes about the painting round,
And who she finds forlorn she doth lament.   *1500*
At last she sees a wretched image bound,   1501
That piteous looks to Phrygian shepherds lent;   1502
His face, though full of cares, yet showed content;
    Onward to Troy with the blunt swains he goes,   1504
    So mild that patience seemed to scorn his woes.

In him the painter labored with his skill
To hide deceit and give the harmless show
An humble gait, calm looks, eyes wailing still,
A brow unbent that seemed to welcome woe;
Cheeks neither red nor pale, but mingled so   *1510*
    That blushing red no guilty instance gave,   1511
    Nor ashy pale the fear that false hearts have.

But like a constant and confirmèd devil,   1513
He entertained a show so seeming just,   1514
And therein so ensconced his secret evil,   1515
That jealousy itself could not mistrust   1516
False creeping craft and perjury should thrust
    Into so bright a day such black-faced storms,
    Or blot with hell-born sin such saintlike forms.

1494 *on ringing* ringing **1497** *penciled* painted, depicted **1501** *image bound* i.e., of a bound man **1502** *Phrygian* Trojan **1504** *blunt swains* common laborers (i.e., the shepherds) **1511** *instance* sign **1513** *constant* steady, unalterable; *confirmèd* settled **1514** *entertained* kept up **1515** *ensconced* housed **1516** *jealousy* suspicion; *mistrust* suspect

1520 The well-skilled workman this mild image drew
1521 For perjured Sinon, whose enchanting story
    The credulous old Priam after slew;
1523 Whose words like wildfire burnt the shining glory
    Of rich-built Ilion, that the skies were sorry,
1525   And little stars shot from their fixèd places,
1526   When their glass fell, wherein they viewed their faces.

This picture she advisedly perused,
And chid the painter for his wondrous skill,
1529 Saying, some shape in Sinon's was abused:
1530 So fair a form lodged not a mind so ill.
And still on him she gazed, and gazing still,
1532   Such signs of truth in his plain face she spied
1533   That she concludes the picture was belied.

"It cannot be," quoth she, "that so much guile" –
She would have said, "can lurk in such a look";
1536 But Tarquin's shape came in her mind the while,
1537 And from her tongue "can lurk" from "cannot" took:
"It cannot be" she in that sense forsook,
    And turned it thus: "It cannot be, I find,
1540   But such a face should bear a wicked mind:

"For even as subtle Sinon here is painted,
1542 So sober-sad, so weary, and so mild,
1543 As if with grief or travel he had fainted,
1544 To me came Tarquin armèd to beguild

1521 *Sinon* the traitor who brought about Troy's destruction by persuading
Priam to admit the wooden horse in which Greek warriors were concealed
1523 *wildfire* explosive mixture used in siege warfare   1525 *fixèd places* fixed
positions in a stable cosmos   1526 *glass* mirror, reflector   1529 *some . . .
abused* someone else's body had been degraded by being used as a model for
Sinon   1532 *plain* honest   1533 *was belied* was falsified   1536 *the while* in
the meantime   1537 *from "cannot" took* i.e., separated from (she cannot join
"can lurk" to "it cannot be that")   1540 *But* otherwise than that   1542 *sad*
serious   1543 *had fainted* was exhausted   1544 *beguild* deceive

With outward honesty, but yet defiled
  With inward vice. As Priam him did cherish,
  So did I Tarquin; so my Troy did perish.

"Look, look, how listening Priam wets his eyes,
To see those borrowed tears that Sinon sheds.
Priam, why art thou old and yet not wise?   1550
For every tear he falls a Trojan bleeds.   1551
His eye drops fire, no water thence proceeds;
  Those round clear pearls of his that move thy pity
  Are balls of quenchless fire to burn thy city.   1554

"Such devils steal effects from lightless hell,
For Sinon in his fire doth quake with cold,
And in that cold hot-burning fire doth dwell.
These contraries such unity do hold
Only to flatter fools and make them bold;
  So Priam's trust false Sinon's tears doth flatter   1560
  That he finds means to burn his Troy with water."

Here, all enraged, such passion her assails
That patience is quite beaten from her breast.
She tears the senseless Sinon with her nails,   1564
Comparing him to that unhappy guest
Whose deed hath made herself herself detest.
  At last she smilingly with this gives o'er:
  "Fool, fool," quoth she, "his wounds will not be sore."

Thus ebbs and flows the current of her sorrow,
And time doth weary time with her complaining;   1570
She looks for night, and then she longs for morrow,
And both she thinks too long with her remaining.

1551 *falls* lets fall   1554 *quenchless* unquenchable   1564 *senseless* unfeeling, insentient

1573 Short time seems long in sorrow's sharp sustaining:
       Though woe be heavy, yet it seldom sleeps,
1575   And they that watch see time how slow it creeps.

1576 Which all this time hath overslipped her thought
       That she with painted images hath spent,
       Being from the feeling of her own grief brought
1579 By deep surmise of others' detriment,
1580 Losing her woes in shows of discontent.
           It easeth some, though none it ever cured,
           To think their dolor others have endured.

1583 But now the mindful messenger come back
       Brings home his lord and other company;
       Who finds his Lucrece clad in mourning black,
1586 And round about her tear-distainèd eye
       Blue circles streamed, like rainbows in the sky:
1588   These water galls in her dim element
         Foretell new storms to those already spent.

1590 Which when her sad beholding husband saw,
       Amazedly in her sad face he stares:
1592 Her eyes, though sod in tears, looked red and raw,
       Her lively color killed with deadly cares.
       He hath no power to ask her how she fares;
           Both stood like old acquaintance in a trance,
1596   Met far from home, wondering each other's chance.

       At last he takes her by the bloodless hand,
1598 And thus begins: "What uncouth ill event
       Hath thee befallen, that thou dost trembling stand?

1573 *in . . . sustaining* while sorrow's pangs have to be borne 1575 *watch*
lie awake 1576 *Which* i.e., her sorrow; *overslipped* slipped out of 1579
surmise consideration; *detriment* misfortune 1583 *mindful* conscientious
1586 *distainèd* stained 1588 *water galls* secondary rainbows; *her dim ele-*
ment the overcast sky of her face 1592 *sod* boiled 1596 *chance* fortunes
1598 *uncouth* unknown

Sweet love, what spite hath thy fair color spent? 1600
Why art thou thus attired in discontent?
   Unmask, dear dear, this moody heaviness,
   And tell thy grief, that we may give redress."

Three times with sighs she gives her sorrow fire
Ere once she can discharge one word of woe;
At length addressed to answer his desire,
She modestly prepares to let them know
Her honor is ta'en prisoner by the foe;
   While Collatine and his consorted lords
   With sad attention long to hear her words. 1610

And now this pale swan in her watery nest 1611
Begins the sad dirge of her certain ending. 1612
"Few words," quoth she, "shall fit the trespass best,
Where no excuse can give the fault amending: 1614
In me moe woes than words are now depending; 1615
   And my laments would be drawn out too long
   To tell them all with one poor tirèd tongue.

"Then be this all the task it hath to say:
Dear husband, in the interest of thy bed 1619
A stranger came, and on that pillow lay 1620
Where thou wast wont to rest thy weary head;
And what wrong else may be imaginèd
   By foul enforcement might be done to me,
   From that, alas, thy Lucrece is not free.

"For in the dreadful dead of dark midnight
With shining falchion in my chamber came 1626
A creeping creature with a flaming light,

1600 *spent* wasted, extinguished 1611–12 *pale . . . ending* (alludes to the belief that the swan utters a beautiful song just before it dies; swan song) 1612 *dirge* mournful song 1614 *give . . . amending* make amends 1615 *moe* more; *depending* impending 1619 *interest of thy bed* i.e., bed rightfully yours 1626 *falchion* sword

And softly cried 'Awake, thou Roman dame,
1629 And entertain my love; else lasting shame
1630   On thee and thine this night I will inflict,
       If thou my love's desire do contradict.

1632 "'For some hard-favored groom of thine,' quoth he,
1633 'Unless thou yoke thy liking to my will,
     I'll murder straight, and then I'll slaughter thee,
     And swear I found you where you did fulfill
     The loathsome act of lust, and so did kill
        The lechers in their deed: this act will be
        My fame, and thy perpetual infamy.'

     "With this I did begin to start and cry,
1640 And then against my heart he set his sword,
     Swearing, unless I took all patiently,
     I should not live to speak another word;
     So should my shame still rest upon record,
        And never be forgot in mighty Rome
1645   Th' adulterate death of Lucrece and her groom.

     "Mine enemy was strong, my poor self weak,
     And far the weaker with so strong a fear.
     My bloody judge forbade my tongue to speak;
     No rightful plea might plead for justice there.
1650 His scarlet lust came evidence to swear
        That my poor beauty had purloined his eyes;
1652   And when the judge is robbed, the prisoner dies.

     "O teach me how to make mine own excuse;
     Or at the least this refuge let me find:
     Though my gross blood be stained with this abuse,
     Immaculate and spotless is my mind;

1629 *entertain* receive 1632 *hard-favored* of brutal appearance 1633
yoke . . . will submit your inclination to my desire 1645 *adulterate* adulter-
ous 1650 *came evidence* bore witness 1652 *robbed* both "robed" and
"robbed of judgment"

That was not forced, that never was inclined   1657
   To accessary yieldings, but still pure   1658
   Doth in her poisoned closet yet endure."   1659

Lo, here the hopeless merchant of this loss,   1660
With head declined and voice dammed up with woe,
With sad set eyes and wretched arms across,
From lips new waxen pale begins to blow
The grief away that stops his answer so;
   But wretched as he is, he strives in vain;
   What he breathes out his breath drinks up again.   1666

As through an arch the violent roaring tide
Outruns the eye that doth behold his haste,
Yet in the eddy boundeth in his pride   1669
Back to the strait that forced him on so fast,   *1670*
In rage sent out, recalled in rage, being past;
   Even so his sighs, his sorrows, make a saw,   1672
   To push grief on and back the same grief draw.

Which speechless woe of his poor she attendeth,
And his untimely frenzy thus awaketh: 1675
"Dear lord, thy sorrow to my sorrow lendeth
Another power; no flood by raining slaketh;
My woe too sensible thy passion maketh   1678
   More feeling-painful. Let it then suffice
   To drown on woe one pair of weeping eyes.   1680

"And for my sake, when I might charm thee so,   1681
For she that was thy Lucrece, now attend me:

1657 *forced* violated   1658 *accessary yieldings* both "yielding access" and "be-coming an accessory"   1659 *poisoned closet* polluted body   1660 *merchant of this loss* i.e., Collatine is like a merchant who has suffered the loss of his in-vestment   1666 *What . . . again* i.e., he cannot speak because his grief makes him gulp down his breath   1669 *boundeth* rebounds   1672 *make a saw* i.e., behave like a saw, moved backward and forward   1675 *untimely* un-fitting, prolonged; *awaketh* interrupts   1678 *sensible* deeply felt   1680 *on* in   1681 *when* while

1683 Be suddenly revengèd on my foe,
1684 Thine, mine, his own. Suppose thou dost defend me
From what is past. The help that thou shalt lend me
    Comes all too late, yet let the traitor die,
    For sparing justice feeds iniquity.

"But ere I name him, you fair lords," quoth she,
Speaking to those that came with Collatine,
1690 "Shall plight your honorable faiths to me,
With swift pursuit to venge this wrong of mine;
For 'tis a meritorious fair design
    To chase injustice with revengeful arms:
    Knights by their oaths should right poor ladies'
      harms."

At this request, with noble disposition
Each present lord began to promise aid,
1697 As bound in knighthood to her imposition,
1698 Longing to hear the hateful foe bewrayed;
1699 But she, that yet her sad task hath not said,
1700   The protestation stops. "O speak," quoth she:
    "How may this forcèd stain be wiped from me?

1702 "What is the quality of my offense,
1703 Being constrained with dreadful circumstance?
1704 May my pure mind with the foul act dispense,
1705 My low-declinèd honor to advance?
1706 May any terms acquit me from this chance?
    The poisoned fountain clears itself again;
1708   And why not I from this compellèd stain?"

1683 *suddenly* immediately 1684 *Suppose* imagine 1690 *plight* pledge
1697 *imposition* imposed task 1698 *bewrayed* revealed 1699 *sad . . . said*
i.e., she has not yet named the aggressor 1700 *protestation* avowal (of will-
ingness to avenge her) 1702 *quality* nature 1703 *constrained* compelled
1704 *dispense* pardon 1705 *advance* rehabilitate 1706 *terms* arguments;
chance circumstance 1708 *compellèd* enforced

With this they all at once began to say
Her body's stain her mind untainted clears,   *1710*
While with a joyless smile she turns away
The face, that map which deep impression bears
Of hard misfortune, carved in it with tears.
　"No, no," quoth she, "no dame hereafter living
　By my excuse shall claim excuse's giving."   1715

Here with a sigh as if her heart would break
She throws forth Tarquin's name: "He, he," she says;
But more than "he" her poor tongue could not speak;
Till after many accents and delays,   1719
Untimely breathings, sick and short assays,   1720
　She utters this: "He, he, fair lords, 'tis he,
　That guides this hand to give this wound to me."

Even here she sheathèd in her harmless breast
A harmful knife, that thence her soul unsheathèd:
That blow did bail it from the deep unrest   1725
Of that polluted prison where it breathèd.
Her contrite sighs unto the clouds bequeathèd   1727
　Her wingèd sprite, and through her wounds doth fly   1728
　Life's lasting date from canceled destiny.   1729

Stone-still, astonished with this deadly deed,   1730
Stood Collatine and all his lordly crew;
Till Lucrece' father, that beholds her bleed,
Himself on her self-slaughtered body threw;
And from the purple fountain Brutus drew
　The murd'rous knife; and, as it left the place,
　Her blood in poor revenge held it in chase.   1736

1715 *By . . . giving* i.e., shall excuse herself because I was excused   1719 *accents* sounds   1720 *assays* attempts   1725 *bail it* set it free   1727 *contrite* remorseful   1728 *sprite* spirit   1729 *Life's lasting date* eternal life; *canceled destiny* mortal life or everlasting misery   1730 *astonished* stunned, petrified   1736 *held it in chase* chased after it

And bubbling from her breast it doth divide
In two slow rivers, that the crimson blood
1739 Circles her body in on every side,
1740 Who like a late-sacked island vastly stood
Bare and unpeopled in this fearful flood.
    Some of her blood still pure and red remained,
    And some looked black, and that false Tarquin
        stained.

About the mourning and congealèd face
1745 Of that black blood a watery rigol goes,
Which seems to weep upon the tainted place;
And ever since, as pitying Lucrece' woes,
Corrupted blood some watery token shows;
1749 And blood untainted still doth red abide,
1750 Blushing at that which is so putrified.

"Daughter, dear daughter," old Lucretius cries,
"That life was mine which thou hast here deprivèd;
If in the child the father's image lies,
1754 Where shall I live now Lucrece is unlivèd?
Thou wast not to this end from me derivèd:
    If children predecease progenitors,
    We are their offspring, and they none of ours.

1758 "Poor broken glass, I often did behold
1759 In thy sweet semblance my old age new born;
1760 But now that fair fresh mirror, dim and old,
Shows me a bare-boned death by time outworn.
O, from thy cheeks my image thou hast torn,
1763 And shivered all the beauty of my glass,
    That I no more can see what once I was.

1739 *Circles . . . in* encircles 1740 *Who* which; *late-sacked* lately conquered
and pillaged 1745 *rigol* ring 1749 *abide* remains 1754 *unlivèd* deprived
of life 1758 *glass* mirror 1759 *semblance* appearance 1763 *shivered* splin-
tered

"O time, cease thou thy course and last no longer,
If they surcease to be that should survive!   1766
Shall rotten death make conquest of the stronger,
And leave the faltering feeble souls alive?
The old bees die, the young possess their hive;
   Then live, sweet Lucrece, live again and see   *1770*
   Thy father die, and not thy father thee!"

By this starts Collatine as from a dream,   1772
And bids Lucretius give his sorrow place;   1773
And then in key-cold Lucrece' bleeding stream
He falls, and bathes the pale fear in his face,
And counterfeits to die with her a space;   1776
   Till manly shame bids him possess his breath,   1777
   And live to be revengèd on her death.

The deep vexation of his inward soul
Hath served a dumb arrest upon his tongue;   1780
Who, mad that sorrow should his use control,   1781
Or keep him from heart-easing words so long,
Begins to talk; but through his lips do throng
   Weak words, so thick come in his poor heart's aid   1784
   That no man could distinguish what he said.

Yet sometime "Tarquin" was pronouncèd plain,
But through his teeth, as if the name he tore.
This windy tempest, till it blow up rain,
Held back his sorrow's tide to make it more.
At last it rains, and busy winds give o'er;   *1790*
   Then son and father weep with equal strife
   Who should weep most, for daughter or for wife.

1766 *surcease* cease   1772 *starts* awakens, regains his senses   1773 *give . . .
place* give precedence to his (Collatine's) sorrow   1776 *a space* for a time
1777 *possess* regain   1780 *Hath . . . arrest* has served a warrant of silence
(i.e., made him speechless)   1781 *his* i.e., the tongue's   1784 *thick come* in
confused abundance

Then one doth call her his, the other his,
1794 Yet neither may possess the claim they lay.
The father says "She's mine"; "O, mine she is,"
Replies her husband; "do not take away
1797 My sorrow's interest; let no mourner say
     He weeps for her, for she was only mine,
     And only must be wailed by Collatine."

1800 "O," quoth Lucretius, "I did give that life
1801 Which she too early and too late hath spilled."
"Woe, woe," quoth Collatine, "she was my wife;
1803 I owed her, and 'tis mine that she hath killed."
"My daughter" and "my wife" with clamors filled
1805   The dispersed air, who, holding Lucrece' life,
     Answered their cries, "my daughter" and "my wife."

Brutus, who plucked the knife from Lucrece' side,
1808 Seeing such emulation in their woe
1809 Began to clothe his wit in state and pride,
1810 Burying in Lucrece' wound his folly's show.
1811 He with the Romans was esteemèd so
     As silly jeering idiots are with kings,
     For sportive words and uttering foolish things.

1814 But now he throws that shallow habit by
Wherein deep policy did him disguise,
And armed his long-hid wits advisedly
To check the tears in Collatinus' eyes.
"Thou wrongèd lord of Rome," quoth he, "arise;
1819   Let my unsounded self, supposed a fool,
1820   Now set thy long-experienced wit to school.

1794 *possess* take possession of   1797 *interest* entitlement   1801 *too late* too
recently   1803 *owed* owned   1805 *dispersed* blown about; *holding . . . life*
i.e., housing her spirit   1808 *emulation* competitiveness   1809 *clothe his
wit* dress up his mind   1810 *folly's show* appearance of being a fool   1811 *es-
teemèd* regarded   1814 *shallow habit* superficial costume   1819 *unsounded*
untested

"Why, Collatine, is woe the cure for woe?
Do wounds help wounds, or grief help grievous deeds?
Is it revenge to give thyself a blow
For his foul act by whom thy fair wife bleeds?
Such childish humor from weak minds proceeds;
   Thy wretched wife mistook the matter so
   To slay herself, that should have slain her foe.

"Courageous Roman, do not steep thy heart
In such relenting dew of lamentations,   1829
But kneel with me and help to bear thy part   *1830*
To rouse our Roman gods with invocations
That they will suffer these abominations –   1832
   Since Rome herself in them doth stand disgraced –
   By our strong arms from forth her fair streets chased.

"Now by the Capitol that we adore,
And by this chaste blood so unjustly stained,
By heaven's fair sun that breeds the fat earth's store,   1837
By all our country rights in Rome maintained,   1838
And by chaste Lucrece' soul that late complained
   Her wrongs to us, and by this bloody knife,   *1840*
   We will revenge the death of this true wife."

This said, he struck his hand upon his breast,
And kissed the fatal knife to end his vow,
And to his protestation urged the rest,   1844
Who, wondering at him, did his words allow.   1845
Then jointly to the ground their knees they bow,
   And that deep vow which Brutus made before
   He doth again repeat, and that they swore.

1829 *relenting* softening   1832 *suffer* permit   1837 *fat* abundant   1838 *country* belonging to the provinces (of Rome)   1844 *protestation* avowal   1845 *allow* accept

1849 When they had sworn to this advisèd doom,
1850 They did conclude to bear dead Lucrece thence,
1851 To show her bleeding body thorough Rome,
     And so to publish Tarquin's foul offense;
     Which being done with speedy diligence,
1854   The Romans plausibly did give consent
         To Tarquin's everlasting banishment.

1849 *advisèd doom* considered decree   1851 *thorough* through   1854 *plausibly* with acclaim

The Phoenix and the Turtle

Let the bird of loudest lay,   1
On the sole Arabian tree,   2
Herald sad and trumpet be,   3
To whose sound chaste wings obey.

But thou, shrieking harbinger,   5
Foul precurrer of the fiend,   6
Augur of the fever's end,   7
To this troop come thou not near!

From this session interdict   9
Every fowl of tyrant wing,   10
Save the eagle, feathered king:
Keep the obsequy so strict.   12

Let the priest in surplice white,   13
That defunctive music can,   14
Be the death-divining swan,   15
Lest the requiem lack his right.   16

---

1 *lay* song 2 *sole Arabian tree* (unique, mythical tree in Arabia in which the
phoenix makes its nest) 3 *trumpet* trumpeter 5 *harbinger* advance herald
(here the screech owl) 6 *precurrer* precursor 7 *Augur* diviner, prophet
(here of death) 9 *session* sitting, proceeding; *interdict* prohibit 10 *tyrant
wing* i.e., raptor 12 *obsequy* mourning rite 13 *surplice* priestly outer gar-
ment (here, swansdown) 14 *defunctive* funeral; *can* knows, can produce
15 *death-divining* foreseeing death (the swan was believed to sing just before
it died—cf. *Lucrece* 1611–12) 16 *requiem* funeral service

17 And thou treble-dated crow,
18 That thy sable gender mak'st
19 With the breath thou giv'st and tak'st,
20 'Mongst our mourners shalt thou go.

21 Here the anthem doth commence:
   Love and constancy is dead;
23 Phoenix and the turtle fled
   In a mutual flame from hence.

25 So they loved, as love in twain
   Had the essence but in one;
27 Two distincts, division none:
28 Number there in love was slain.

   Hearts remote, yet not asunder;
30 Distance, and no space was seen
   'Twixt this turtle and his queen:
32 But in them it were a wonder.

   So between them love did shine,
34 That the turtle saw his right
   Flaming in the phoenix' sight;
   Either was the other's mine.

37 Property was thus appalled,
38 That the self was not the same;

---

17 *treble-dated* living three times the normal span (a myth about crows)   18
sable gender black offspring   19 *With . . . tak'st* (myth that crows are insemi-
nated and reproduce through their beaks)   21 *anthem* praise-song   23 *tur-
tle* turtledove   25–26 *as . . . one* as if the love between two creatures united
them into one being containing the essence of love   27 *Two . . . none* a sep-
arate but undivided pair   28 *Number . . . slain* numbering was annulled
since one alone is no number   32 *But . . . wonder* except in their case, it
would be a miracle   34 *right* property, essential quality   37 *Property* both
ownership and the uniqueness of the self; what is proper or peculiar to it
38 *the same* identical to itself

Single nature's double name   39
Neither two nor one was called.   40

Reason, in itself confounded,   41
Saw division grow together,   42
To themselves yet either neither,
Simple were so well compounded;   44

That it cried, How true a twain
Seemeth this concordant one!   46
Love hath reason, reason none,   47
If what parts can so remain.   48

Whereupon it made this threne   49
To the phoenix and the dove,   50
Co-supremes and stars of love,
As chorus to their tragic scene.

THRENOS

Beauty, truth, and rarity,   53
Grace in all simplicity,
Here enclosed, in cinders lie.

Death is now the phoenix' nest;
And the turtle's loyal breast
To eternity doth rest.

39–40 *Single . . . called* that which has become single still has a double name
(phoenix and turtle) and cannot be called double or single **41** *Reason . . .
confounded* reason, contradicted or confused in its own terms **42** *Saw . . .
together* saw what is categorically distinct unite **44** *Simple* single elements
46 *concordant one* a "one" produced by the deep, convergent affinity of two
47 *Love . . . none* love at once defeats and represents (possesses) reason **48**
what . . . remain what is separate (divided) can remain single **49** *threne*
dirge, threnody **53** *rarity* specialness

Leaving no posterity,
60 'Twas not their infirmity,
It was married chastity.

Truth may seem, but cannot be;
Beauty brag, but 'tis not she;
Truth and beauty buried be.

65 To this urn let those repair
That are either true or fair;
For these dead birds sigh a prayer.

---

60 *infirmity* bodily incapacity   **65** *repair* come in devotion

The Passionate Pilgrim

1

When my love swears that she is made of truth,
I do believe her, though I know she lies,
That she might think me some untutored youth,
Unskillful in the world's false forgeries.   4
Thus vainly thinking that she thinks me young,
Although I know my years be past the best,
I smiling credit her false-speaking tongue,
Outfacing faults in love with love's ill rest.   8
But wherefore says my love that she is young?
And wherefore say not I that I am old?   10
O, love's best habit is a soothing tongue,   11
And age in love loves not to have years told.   12
    Therefore I'll lie with love, and love with me,   13
    Since that our faults in love thus smothered be.

1

A version of Shakespeare's Sonnet 138 (1609). Although this version was
first published in 1599, it may have been written earlier or later than the
1609 version, since dates of publication do not necessarily indicate the time
or sequence of composition. This poem differs significantly from Sonnet
138; editors and critics have frequently pursued comparisons.   4 *Unskillful*
uninitiated, incompetent; *forgeries* deceits   8 *Outfacing* braving, denying; *ill
rest* imperfect sense of security   11 *habit* practice, garb   12 *told* divulged,
counted up   13 *lie* tell lies, sleep with

2

Two loves I have, of comfort and despair,
2 That like two spirits do suggest me still;
My better angel is a man right fair,
My worser spirit a woman colored ill.
5 To win me soon to hell, my female evil
Tempteth my better angel from my side,
And would corrupt my saint to be a devil,
Wooing his purity with her fair pride.
And whether that my angel be turned fiend,
10 Suspect I may, yet not directly tell;
For being both to me, both to each friend,
I guess one angel in another's hell.
    The truth I shall not know, but live in doubt,
14   Till my bad angel fire my good one out.

3

Did not the heavenly rhetoric of thine eye,
2 'Gainst whom the world could not hold argument,
Persuade my heart to this false perjury?
Vows for thee broke deserve not punishment.
5 A woman I forswore; but I will prove,
Thou being a goddess, I forswore not thee:
My vow was earthly, thou a heavenly love;
Thy grace being gained cures all disgrace in me.
My vow was breath, and breath a vapor is;
10 Then thou, fair sun, that on this earth doth shine,

2

A version of Sonnet 144, differing less from the 1609 version than does the previous poem. 2 *suggest* tempt and/or exhort 5 *hell* (allusion to female genitalia) 14 *fire . . . out* infect with syphilis

3

A version of a sonnet spoken by Longaville in *Love's Labor's Lost*, IV.3. Again, differences between the versions are slight. 2 *whom* which 5 *foreswore* renounced

Exhal'st this vapor vow; in thee it is: 11
If broken, then it is no fault of mine.
   If by me broke, what fool is not so wise
   To break an oath, to win a paradise?

4

Sweet Cytherea, sitting by a brook   1
With young Adonis, lovely, fresh and green,
Did court the lad with many a lovely look,   3
Such looks as none could look but beauty's queen.
She told him stories to delight his ear;
She showed him favors to allure his eye;   6
To win his heart, she touched him here and there;
Touches so soft still conquer chastity.
But whether unripe years did want conceit,   9
Or he refused to take her figured proffer,   10
The tender nibbler would not touch the bait,
But smile and jest at every gentle offer:
   Then fell she on her back, fair queen, and toward: 13
   He rose and ran away – ah, fool too froward.   14

5

If love make me forsworn, how shall I swear to love?   1
O, never faith could hold, if not to beauty vowed:
Though to myself forsworn, to thee I'll constant prove;

---

11 *Exhal'st* (you) draw up; *in . . . is* (now) it is in you
    4
  1 *Cytherea* Venus (compare *Venus and Adonis*)   **3** *lovely* loving   **6** *favors*
love signs   **9** *unripe* youthful, inexperienced; *did want conceit* lacked under-
standing   **10** *figured proffer* the offer of herself she signaled   **13** *toward* will-
ingly, invitingly   **14** *froward* averse
    5
  A poem in hexameters, unlike the more usual pentameters of Shake-
speare's sonnets. Compare *Love's Labor's Lost,* IV.2.   **1** *forsworn* perjured

4 Those thoughts, to me like oaks, to thee like osiers bowed.
5 Study his bias leaves, and make his book thine eyes,
6 Where all those pleasures live that art can comprehend.
7 If knowledge be the mark, to know thee shall suffice;
Well learnèd is that tongue that well can thee commend:
All ignorant that soul that sees thee without wonder;
10 Which is to me some praise, that I thy parts admire.
11 Thine eye Jove's lightning seems, thy voice his dreadful
    thunder,
12 Which, not to anger bent, is music and sweet fire.
    Celestial as thou art, O do not love that wrong,
    To sing heaven's praise with such an earthly tongue.

6

Scarce had the sun dried up the dewy morn,
2 And scarce the herd gone to the hedge for shade,
When Cytherea, all in love forlorn,
4 A longing tarriance for Adonis made
Under an osier growing by a brook,
6 A brook where Adon used to cool his spleen.
Hot was the day; she hotter that did look
For his approach, that often there had been.
Anon he comes, and throws his mantle by,
10 And stood stark naked on the brook's green brim:
The sun looked on the world with glorious eye,
12 Yet not so wistly as this queen on him.
13   He, spying her, bounced in whereas he stood.
14   "O Jove," quoth she, "why was not I a flood!"

---

4 *osiers* willows 5 *Study . . . leaves* studiousness abandons its natural inclina-
tion 6 *comprehend* understand, include 7 *mark* goal 11 *Jove* (in Roman
mythology, king of the gods and wielder of thunderbolts) 12 *bent* turned

6
2 *hedge* hedgerow 4 *tarriance* wait 6 *spleen* annoyance 12 *wistly* desir-
ingly, intently 13 *bounced . . . stood* jumped in where he was standing 14
flood stream

7

Fair is my love, but not so fair as fickle;
Mild as a dove, but neither true nor trusty;
Brighter than glass, and yet, as glass is, brittle;
Softer than wax, and yet as iron rusty;   4
 A lily pale, with damask dye to grace her;   5
 None fairer, nor none falser to deface her.   6

Her lips to mine how often hath she joinèd,
Between each kiss her oaths of true love swearing;
How many tales to please me hath she coinèd,   9
Dreading my love, the loss thereof still fearing.   10
 Yet in the midst of all her pure protestings,
 Her faith, her oaths, her tears, and all were jestings.

She burnt with love, as straw with fire flameth;
She burnt out love, as soon as straw out-burneth;
She framed the love, and yet she foiled the framing;   15
She bade love last, and yet she fell a-turning.   16
 Was this a lover or a lecher, whether?   17
 Bad in the best, though excellent in neither.

8

"If Music and Sweet Poetry Agree" by Richard Barnfield.
From *Poems: In Divers Humors,* added to *The Encomiom
of Lady Pecunia* (1598).

7

4 *iron rusty* i.e., both hard and corroded 5 *damask* blush-red 6 *deface* discredit 9 *coinèd* forged 15 *framed* created; *foiled* spoiled 16 *fell a-turning* became treacherous or unfaithful 17 *whether* which of the two

9

Fair was the morn, when the fair queen of love,

    *   *   *   *   *   *   *

Paler for sorrow than her milk-white dove,
For Adon's sake, a youngster proud and wild.
5 Her stand she takes upon a steep-up hill;
Anon Adonis comes with horn and hounds;
7 She, silly queen, with more than love's good will,
Forbade the boy he should not pass those grounds.
"Once," quoth she, "did I see a fair sweet youth
10 Here in these brakes deep-wounded with a boar,
11 Deep in the thigh, a spectacle of ruth.
12 See, in my thigh," quoth she, "here was the sore."
    She showèd hers; he saw more wounds than one,
    And blushing fled, and left her all alone.

10

1 Sweet rose, fair flower, untimely plucked, soon vaded,
Plucked in the bud and vaded in the spring;
3 Bright orient pearl, alack, too timely shaded,
Fair creature, killed too soon by death's sharp sting;
Like a green plum that hangs upon a tree,
And falls through wind before the fall should be.

I weep for thee and yet no cause I have;
8 For why thou lefts me nothing in thy will.
And yet thou lefts me more than I did crave,
10 For why I cravèd nothing of thee still:
    O yes, dear friend, I pardon crave of thee,
    Thy discontent thou didst bequeath to me.

9
5 *steep-up* rising steeply **7** *silly* simple **10** *brakes* thickets **11** *spectacle of ruth* pitiable sight **12** *sore* wound
10
1 *vaded* faded **3** *orient* of superior quality, from the east; *shaded* dulled **8** *For why* because

11

"Venus with Young Adonis Sitting by Her" by Bartholomew Griffin. From *Fidessa* (1596).

12

Crabbèd age and youth cannot live together: 1
Youth is full of pleasance, age is full of care;   2
Youth like summer morn, age like winter weather;
Youth like summer brave, age like winter bare.
Youth is full of sport, age's breath is short;
   Youth is nimble, age is lame;
Youth is hot and bold, age is weak and cold;
   Youth is wild, and age is tame.
Age, I do abhor thee; youth, I do adore thee;
   O, my love, my love is young!   10
Age, I do defy thee. O, sweet shepherd, hie thee,   11
   For methinks thou stays too long.   12

13

Beauty is but a vain and doubtful good,
A shining gloss that vadeth suddenly,   2
A flower that dies when first it 'gins to bud,
A brittle glass that's broken presently;
   A doubtful good, a gloss, a glass, a flower,   5
   Lost, vaded, broken, dead within an hour.

And as goods lost are seld or never found,   7
As vaded gloss no rubbing will refresh,
As flowers dead lie withered on the ground,

12
1 *Crabbèd* narrow, irritable **2** *pleasance* delight **11** *hie thee* hurry **12** *stays* tarries
13
2 *vadeth* fades **5** *gloss* shiny surface **7** *seld* seldom

10 As broken glass no cement can redress:
    So beauty blemished once, forever lost,
12   In spite of physic, painting, pain and cost.

14

Good night, good rest: ah, neither be my share;
She bade good night that kept my rest away;
3 And daffed me to a cabin hanged with care,
4 To descant on the doubts of my decay.
    "Farewell," quoth she, "and come again tomorrow."
    Fare well I could not, for I supped with sorrow.

Yet at my parting sweetly did she smile,
8 In scorn or friendship nill I conster whether;
'T may be she joyed to jest at my exile,
10 'T may be again to make me wander thither:
    "Wander," a word for shadows like myself,
12   As take the pain, but cannot pluck the pelf.

Lord, how mine eyes throw gazes to the east!
14 My heart doth charge the watch; the morning rise
15 Doth cite each moving sense from idle rest.
16 Not daring trust the office of mine eyes,
17   While Philomela sings, I sit and mark,
18   And wish her lays were tunèd like the lark.

For she doth welcome daylight with her ditty,
20 And drives away dark dreaming night.
21 The night so packed, I post unto my pretty;

---

10 *redress* repair   12 *physic* medicine; *painting* application of cosmetics
  14
3 *daffed* banished; *cabin* hut, lodge; *hanged* curtained   4 *descant* sing, expatiate upon; *doubts* fears   8 *nill I conster whether* I cannot interpret which   12 *As . . . pain* i.e., such as endure the pain and/or take pains; *pluck the pelf* reap the reward   14 *charge the watch* make waiting anxious (?)   15 *cite* summon; *moving* living   16 *office* function   17 *Philomela* the nightingale; *mark* listen   18 *lays* songs   21 *packed* sent packing; *post* hasten

Heart hath his hope and eyes their wishèd sight;
  Sorrow changed to solace, and solace mixed with
    sorrow,
  For why she sighed, and bade me come tomorrow.   24

Were I with her, the night would post too soon,
But now are minutes added to the hours;
To spite me now, each minute seems a moon;   27
Yet not for me, shine sun to succor flowers!
  Pack night, peep day; good day, of night now borrow;   29
  Short night, tonight, and length thyself tomorrow.   30

15

It was a lording's daughter, the fairest one of three,   1
That likèd of her master as well as well might be,   2
Till looking on an Englishman, the fairest that eye
  could see,
  Her fancy fell a-turning.
Long was the combat doubtful that love with love did
  fight,
To leave the master loveless, or kill the gallant knight;
To put in practice either, alas, it was a spite   7
  Unto the silly damsel!   8
But one must be refusèd; more mickle was the pain   9
That nothing could be usèd to turn them both to gain,   10
For of the two the trusty knight was wounded with
  disdain:
  Alas, she could not help it!
Thus art with arms contending was victor of the day,
Which by a gift of learning did bear the maid away:

---

24 *For why* because   27 *moon* month   29 *Pack* depart; *peep* show forth   30
length lengthen
  15
1 *lording* minor lord, gentleman   2 *master* teacher   7 *a spite* a hardship   8
silly simple   9 *more mickle* greater   10 *usèd* done

Then, lullaby, the learned man hath got the lady gay;
　　For now my song is ended.

16

1 On a day, alack the day!
　Love, whose month was ever May,
3 Spied a blossom passing fair,
　Playing in the wanton air.
　Through the velvet leaves the wind
　All unseen 'gan passage find,
　That the lover, sick to death,
　Wished himself the heaven's breath.
　"Air," quoth he, "thy cheeks may blow;
10 Air, would I might triumph so!
　But, alas! my hand hath sworn
　Ne'er to pluck thee from thy throne.
13 Vow, alack! for youth umeet,
14 　Youth so apt to pluck a sweet.
15 　Thou for whom Jove would swear
16 　Juno but an Ethiope were;
17 　And deny himself for Jove,
　　Turning mortal for thy love."

17

My flocks feed not, my ewes breed not,
2 My rams speed not, all is amiss;
　Love is dying, faith's defying,
　Heart's denying, causer of this.
　All my merry jigs are quite forgot,
6 All my lady's love is lost, God wot;

16

A version of Dumaine's sonnet in *Loves' Labor's Lost,* IV.2.95–96. **1** *alack* alas
3 *passing fair* surpassingly beautiful **13** *unmeet* inappropriate **14** *sweet*
sweetmeat **15** *Jove* king of the gods in Roman mythology **16** *Juno* wife of
Jove; *Ethiope* Ethiopian **17** *for* i.e., as
17
2 *speed* prosper **6** *wot* knows

Where her faith was firmly fixed in love,
There a nay is placed without remove.
    One silly cross wrought all my loss;   9
    O frowning fortune, cursèd fickle dame!   10
    For now I see inconstancy
    More in women than in men remain.

In black mourn I, all fears scorn I,
Love hath forlorn me, living in thrall: 14
Heart is bleeding, all help needing,
O cruel speeding, fraughted with gall.   16
My shepherd's pipe can sound no deal;   17
My wether's bell rings doleful knell;   18
My curtal dog that wont to have played,   19
Plays not at all, but seems afraid;   20
    With sighs so deep procures to weep,
    In howling wise, to see my doleful plight.
    How sighs resound through heartless ground,   23
    Like a thousand vanquished men in bloody fight!

Clear wells spring not, sweet birds sing not,
Green plants bring not forth their dye;   26
Herds stand weeping, flocks all sleeping,
Nymphs back peeping fearfully.
All our pleasure known to us poor swains,
All our merry meetings on the plains,   30
All our evening sport from us is fled,
All our love is lost, for love is dead.
    Farewell, sweet lass, thy like ne'er was
    For a sweet content, the cause of all my woe:
    Poor Corydon must live alone;   35
    Other help for him I see that there is none.

---

9 *cross* quarrel **14** *thrall* bondage **16** *speeding* fortune; *fraughted* loaded **17** *no deal* i.e., not a great deal, not at all **18** *wether* castrated sheep **19** *curtal* with a docked tail **23** *heartless ground* forlorn, unresponding landscape **26** *dye* color **35** *Corydon* (typical shepherd name in classical pastoral poetry since Virgil)

18

When as thine eye hath chose the dame,
2 And stalled the deer that thou shouldst strike,
3 Let reason rule things worthy blame,
As well as fancy, partial might;
    Take counsel of some wiser head,
    Neither too young nor yet unwed.

And when thou com'st thy tale to tell,
8 Smooth not thy tongue with filèd talk,
9 Lest she some subtle practice smell –
10 A cripple soon can find a halt –
    But plainly say thou lov'st her well,
12   And set her person forth to sale.

13 And to her will frame all thy ways;
Spare not to spend, and chiefly there
Where thy desert may merit praise,
By ringing in thy lady's ear:
    The strongest castle, tower and town,
    The golden bullet beats it down.

Serve always with assurèd trust,
20 And in thy suit be humble true;
21 Unless thy lady prove unjust,
Press never thou to choose a new:
    When time shall serve, be thou not slack
24   To proffer, though she put thee back.

What though her frowning brows be bent,
Her cloudy looks will calm ere night,

18
2 *stalled* brought to a halt   3–4 *Let . . . might* let (impartial) reason rule over blameworthy things as well as (rather than) the partial power of fantasy 8 *filèd* smooth, polished   9 *practice* deception   10 *halt* lame person   12 *set . . . sale* extol her charms, as to a buyer   13 *frame* shape, adapt   21 *unjust* untrue   24 *proffer* put yourself forward

And then too late she will repent
That thus dissembled her delight;
    And twice desire, ere it be day,
    That which with scorn she put away.   *30*

What though she strive to try her strength,
And ban and brawl, and say thee nay,   *32*
Her feeble force will yield at length,
When craft hath taught her thus to say:
    "Had women been so strong as men,
    In faith, you had not had it then."   *36*

The wiles and guiles that women work,
Dissembled with an outward show,
The tricks and toys that in them lurk,   *39*
The cock that treads them shall not know.   *40*
    Have you not heard it said full oft,
    A woman's nay doth stand for nought?   *42*

Think women still to strive with men,
To sin and never for to saint: *44*
There is no heaven; be holy then,
When time with age shall them attaint.   *46*
    Were kisses all the joys in bed,
    One woman would another wed.

But soft, enough, too much I fear,
Lest that my mistress hear my song;   *50*
She will not stick to round me on th' ear,   *51*
To teach my tongue to be so long,
    Yet will she blush, here be it said,
    To hear her secrets so bewrayed.

---

32 *ban* curse; *brawl* make an uproar 36 *had not had* would not have had
39 *toys* whims 40 *treads* sexually mounts 42 *for nought* for nothing, but
implying sexual willingness ("naughtiness") as well as female genitalia 44 *to
saint* to be pure or holy 46 *attaint* spoil the looks of 51 *round* strike

19

"Live with Me and Be My Love" and "Love's Answer" by Christopher Marlowe and Walter Ralegh, respectively.

20

"As It Fell upon a Day" by Richard Barnfield. From *Poems: In Divers Humors,* added to *The Encomiom of Lady Pecunia* (1598).

A Lover's Complaint

From off a hill whose concave womb re-worded   1
A plaintful story from a sist'ring vale,   2
My spirits t' attend this double voice accorded,   3
And down I laid to list the sad-tuned tale;
Ere long espied a fickle maid full pale,   5
Tearing of papers, breaking rings a-twain,   6
Storming her world with sorrow's wind and rain.

Upon her head a platted hive of straw,   8
Which fortified her visage from the sun,
Whereon the thought might think sometime it saw   10
The carcass of a beauty spent and done.   11
Time had not scythèd all that youth begun,   12
Nor youth all quit; but, spite of heaven's fell rage, 13
Some beauty peeped through lattice of seared age.   14

Oft did she heave her napkin to her eyne,   15
Which on it had conceited characters,   16
Laund'ring the silken figures in the brine
That seasoned woe had pelleted in tears,   18
And often reading what contents it bears;

---

1 *womb re-worded* i.e., valley reechoed   2 *sist'ring* i.e., matching (one similar and nearby)   3 *accorded* inclined   5 *fickle* changeable, perturbed   6 *papers* love letters   8 *platted hive* woven hat   10 *thought* mind   11 *carcass* remnant   12 *scythèd* cut down   13 *all quit* entirely gone; *fell* deadly   14 *lattice* wrinkled visage   15 *heave* lift; *napkin* handkerchief   16 *conceited* ingenious   18 *seasoned* (1) matured, (2) salted (punning on "brine"); *pelleted* (1) rounded, (2) prepared as seasoners (punning on "pellet" as culinary term)

20 As often shrieking undistinguished woe
    In clamors of all size, both high and low.

22 Sometime her leveled eyes their carriage ride,
23 As they did batt'ry to the spheres intend;
    Sometimes diverted their poor balls are tied
25 To th' orbèd earth; sometimes they do extend
26 Their view right on; anon their gazes lend
    To every place at once, and, nowhere fixed,
    The mind and sight distractedly commixed.

29 Her hair, nor loose nor tied in formal plat,
30 Proclaimed in her a careless hand of pride;
31 For some, untucked, descended her sheaved hat,
    Hanging her pale and pinèd cheek beside;
33 Some in her threaden fillet still did bide
    And, true to bondage, would not break from thence,
    Though slackly braided in loose negligence.

36 A thousand favors from a maund she drew,
37 Of amber, crystal, and of bedded jet,
    Which one by one she in a river threw,
39 Upon whose weeping margent she was set,
40 Like usury, applying wet to wet,
41 Or monarch's hands that lets not bounty fall
    Where want cries some but where excess begs all.

43 Of folded schedules had she many a one
    Which she perused, sighed, tore, and gave the flood;

---

20 *undistinguished* indiscriminate 22 *leveled* (1) directed, (2) aimed; *car-riage ride* move (punning on "gun carriage") 23 *As* as if; *batt'ry . . . spheres* i.e., direct fire against the heavenly bodies (continuing the artillery metaphor) 25 *orbèd* globelike 26 *right on* straight ahead 29 *plat* plait 31 *sheaved* straw 33 *threaden fillet* i.e., ribbon circling the head 36 *favors* love tokens; *maund* basket 37 *bedded* inlaid 39 *weeping margent* wet bank; *set* seated 40 *like usury* i.e., tears breeding more tears 41–42 *Or . . . all* i.e., like kings who do not give to the needy but to the greedy rich 43 *schedules* letters

Cracked many a ring of posied gold and bone,   45
Bidding them find their sepulchers in mud;
Found yet moe letters sadly penned in blood,   47
With sleided silk feat and affectedly   48
Enswathed and sealed to curious secrecy.   49

These often bathed she in her fluxive eyes,   50
And often kissed, and often gave to tear;   51
Cried, "O false blood, thou register of lies,
What unapprovèd witness dost thou bear!   53
Ink would have seemed more black and damnèd here!"
This said, in top of rage the lines she rents,   55
Big discontent so breaking their contents.

A reverend man that grazed his cattle nigh,   57
Sometime a blusterer that the ruffle knew   58
Of court, of city, and had let go by   59
The swiftest hours, observèd as they flew,   60
Towards this afflicted fancy fastly drew,   61
And, privileged by age, desires to know
In brief the grounds and motives of her woe.

So slides he down upon his grainèd bat,   64
And comely-distant sits he by her side;   65
When he again desires her, being sat,
Her grievance with his hearing to divide: 67
If that from him there may be aught applied
Which may her suffering ecstasy assuage,   69
'Tis promised in the charity of age.   70

---

45 *posied* i.e., inscribed with love mottoes   47 *moe* more   48 *sleided* raveled;
feat and affectedly neatly and lovingly   49 *curious* fastidious   50 *fluxive* flow-
ing   51 *gave* i.e., shared an impulse   53 *unapprovèd* unconfirmed   55 *rents*
tears   57 *reverend* aged   58 *blusterer* rambunctious man of the world; *ruffle*
pretentious bustle   59–60 *had . . . flew* had gained knowledge through ob-
servation during the brief time of youth   61 *fancy* i.e., lady in her lovesick
mood; *fastly* closely (?), quickly (?)   64 *grainèd bat* shepherd's staff (so worn
as to show the grain)   65 *comely-distant* i.e., at appropriate distance   67 *di-
vide* share   69 *ecstasy* fit

"Father," she says, "though in me you behold
72 The injury of many a blasting hour,
Let it not tell your judgment I am old;
Not age, but sorrow, over me hath power:
I might as yet have been a spreading flower,
Fresh to myself, if I had self-applied
Love to myself and to no love beside.

78 "But, woe is me, too early I attended
A youthful suit – it was to gain my grace –
80 Of one by nature's outwards so commended
81 That maidens' eyes stuck over all his face:
Love lacked a dwelling, and made him her place;
And when in his fair parts she did abide,
She was new lodged and newly deified.

"His browny locks did hang in crooked curls,
86 And every light occasion of the wind
87 Upon his lips their silken parcels hurls.
88 What's sweet to do, to do will aptly find:
Each eye that saw him did enchant the mind,
90 For on his visage was in little drawn
91 What largeness thinks in paradise was sawn.

"Small show of man was yet upon his chin;
93 His phoenix down began but to appear,
94 Like unshorn velvet, on that termless skin
95 Whose bare outbragged the web it seemed to wear.
96 Yet showed his visage by that cost more dear;

---

72 *blasting* blighting   78 *attended* gave attention to   80 *outwards* appear-
ances   81 *stuck over* attached themselves   86 *occasion* movement   87
parcels parts   88 *What's . . . find* what's pleasant to do is readily done   90 *in
little* in miniature   91 *largeness thinks* what God's design or our most exten-
sive thought conceives; *sawn* seen, sown   93 *phoenix down* i.e., incipient
beard   94 *termless* i.e., young   95 *outbragged* outbraved   96 *by that cost* by
that expense, for that very reason

And nice affections wavering stood in doubt   97
If best were as it was, or best without.

"His qualities were beauteous as his form,
For maiden-tongued he was, and thereof free;   100
Yet, if men moved him, was he such a storm
As oft 'twixt May and April is to see,
When winds breathe sweet, unruly though they be.
His rudeness so with his authorized youth   104
Did livery falseness in a pride of truth.   105

"Well could he ride, and often men would say,
'That horse his mettle from his rider takes.
Proud of subjection, noble by the sway,   108
What rounds, what bounds, what course, what stop he
     makes!'
And controversy hence a question takes,   *110*
Whether the horse by him became his deed,   111
Or he his manage by th' well-doing steed.   112

"But quickly on this side the verdict went: 113
His real habitude gave life and grace   114
To appertainings and to ornament,   115
Accomplished in himself, not in his case.   116
All aids, themselves made fairer by their place,   117
Came for additions; yet their purposed trim   118
Pieced not his grace but were all graced by him.   119

---

97 *nice affections* fastidious taste   100 *maiden-tongued* modest-spoken; *free* innocent   104 *His rudeness so* his turbulent behavior then; *authorized* privileged   105 *livery falseness,* i.e., cloak or conceal indecorousness   108 *by the sway* being controlled   111 *by . . . deed* was exalted because of him   112 *his . . . steed* i.e., excelled in horsemanship because of the skill of the steed   113 *this* the following   114 *real habitude* regal demeanor   115 *appertainings* things associated with him   116 *case* outsides   117 *aids* forms of adornment   118 *Came for additions* were graced by him; *yet . . . trim* their intended embellishment   119 *Pieced* improved

120 "So on the tip of his subduing tongue
     All kinds of arguments and question deep,
122 All replication prompt and reason strong,
123 For his advantage still did wake and sleep.
     To make the weeper laugh, the laugher weep,
125 He had the dialect and different skill,
126 Catching all passions in his craft of will;

127 "That he did in the general bosom reign
128 Of young, of old, and sexes both enchanted
     To dwell with him in thoughts, or to remain
130 In personal duty, following where he haunted.
131 Consents bewitched, ere he desire, have granted,
132 And dialogued for him what he would say,
133 Asked their own wills and made their wills obey.

     "Many there were that did his picture get,
135 To serve their eyes, and in it put their mind;
136 Like fools that in th' imagination set
     The goodly objects which abroad they find
     Of lands and mansions, theirs in thought assigned,
139 And laboring in moe pleasures to bestow them
140 Than the true gouty landlord which doth owe them.

     "So many have, that never touched his hand,
     Sweetly supposed them mistress of his heart.
     My woeful self, that did in freedom stand
144 And was my own fee simple, not in part,
     What with his art in youth and youth in art,

---

120 *subduing* masterful   122 *replication prompt* quick rejoinders   123 *wake and sleep* flow and ebb   125 *dialect* discourse; *different* varying   126 *craft of will* power of persuasion   127 *That* so that   128 *enchanted* charmed, i.e., influenced   130 *haunted* frequented   131 *Consents bewitched* those captivated by his persuasion   132 *dialogued . . . say* spoke his part as well as their own   133 *Asked* made demands upon   135 *put their mind* projected themselves into it   136 *set* set forth   139 *laboring . . . them* i.e., laboring to extract more pleasure from them   140 *gouty* rheumatic (i.e., old); *owe* own   144 *my . . . part* i.e., wholly, not partly, at my own disposal (like land that is freehold)

Threw my affections in his charmèd power,
Reserved the stalk and gave him all my flower.

"Yet did I not, as some my equals did,   148
Demand of him, nor being desirèd yielded.   149
Finding myself in honor so forbid,   150
With safest distance I mine honor shielded.
Experience for me many bulwarks builded   152
Of proofs new-bleeding, which remained the foil   153
Of this false jewel, and his amorous spoil.

"But, ah, whoever shunned by precedent   155
The destined ill she must herself assay?
Or forced examples, 'gainst her own content,   157
To put the by-past perils in her way?   158
Counsel may stop awhile what will not stay;   159
For when we rage, advice is often seen   160
By blunting us to make our wits more keen.   161

"Nor gives it satisfaction to our blood   162
That we must curb it upon others' proof,   163
To be forbod the sweets that seems so good   164
For fear of harms that preach in our behoof.   165
O appetite, from judgment stand aloof!   166
The one a palate hath that needs will taste,
Though reason weep and cry, 'It is thy last.'

---

148 *my equals* i.e., those like me, my kind   149 *Demand . . . yielded* ask, or
yield being asked   152 *Experience* knowledge, awareness; *bulwarks* restraints
153 *proofs new-bleeding* i.e., persons recently victimized; *foil* i.e., dark ground
against which he shone   155 *precedent* example   157 *forced* strongly urged;
content presumed satisfaction   158 *To . . . way* i.e., to raise as obstacles the
past perils (of others)   159 *stop awhile* i.e., only check   160 *rage* i.e., are
aroused   161 *By . . . keen* i.e., to sharpen our wits by opposition (with
blunting us used in a forced antithesis)   162 *blood* passion   163 *proof* exam-
ple   164 *forbod* forbidden   165 *harms . . . behoof* i.e., dangers that give
good counsel   166 *stand aloof* i.e., remain ever unreconciled

169 "For further I could say this man's untrue,
170 And knew the patterns of his foul beguiling;
171 Heard where his plants in others' orchards grew;
Saw how deceits were gilded in his smiling;
173 Knew vows were ever brokers to defiling;
174 Thought characters and words merely but art,
175 And bastards of his foul adulterate heart.

176 "And long upon these terms I held my city,
Till thus he 'gan besiege me: 'Gentle maid,
Have of my suffering youth some feeling pity
And be not of my holy vows afraid.
180 That's to ye sworn to none was ever said;
181 For feasts of love I have been called unto,
Till now did ne'er invite nor never woo.

"'All my offenses that abroad you see
Are errors of the blood, none of the mind.
185 Love made them not; with acture they may be,
Where neither party is nor true nor kind.
They sought their shame that so their shame did find;
And so much less of shame in me remains.
189 By how much of me their reproach contains.

190 "'Among the many that mine eyes have seen,
Not one whose flame my heart so much as warmed,
192 Or my affection put to th' smallest teen,
Or any of my leisures ever charmed.
Harm have I done to them, but ne'er was harmed;
195 Kept hearts in liveries, but mine own was free
And reigned commanding in his monarchy.

---

169 *say . . . untrue* tell of this man's untruth 171 *plants* i.e., bastard off-
spring; *orchards* gardens 173 *brokers* panders 174 *characters and words*
written and spoken words 175 *bastards* base offspring 176 *city* i.e., citadel
of chastity 180 *That's* what's 181 *called unto* invited, solicited 185 *acture*
mechanical action 189 *By . . . contains* the more they reproach me 192
teen distress 195 *liveries* garments of service

"'Look here what tributes wounded fancies sent me   197
Of pallid pearls and rubies red as blood,   198
Figuring that they their passions likewise lent me
Of grief and blushes, aptly understood   *200*
In bloodless white and the encrimsoned mood –   201
Effects of terror and dear modesty,
Encamped in hearts, but fighting outwardly.

"'And, lo, behold these talents of their hair,   204
With twisted metal amorously empleached,   205
I have received from many a several fair,   206
Their kind acceptance weepingly beseeched,
With th' annexions of fair gems enriched,   208
And deep-brained sonnets that did amplify   209
Each stone's dear nature, worth, and quality.   *210*

"'The diamond – why, 'twas beautiful and hard,
Whereto his invised properties did tend;   212
The deep-green em'rald, in whose fresh regard   213
Weak sights their sickly radiance do amend;   214
The heaven-hued sapphire, and the opal blend   215
With objects manifold: each several stone,
With wit well blazoned, smiled or made some moan.   217

"'Lo, all these trophies of affections hot,   218
Of pensived and subdued desires the tender,   219
Nature hath charged me that I hoard them not,   *220*
But yield them up where I myself must render:
That is, to you, my origin and ender;   222

---

197 *fancies* desires; loving women   198 *pallid* pale   201 *mood* guise   204 *talents* golden riches   205 *empleached* entwined   206 *many . . . fair* many different fair ones   208 *annexions* additions (to the gold settings of the locks of hair)   209 *deep-brained* learned; *amplify* expatiate upon   212 *invised* unseen   213 *regard* aspect   214 *radiance* power of vision   215–16 *blend . . . manifold* with the blended colors of many objects (?)   217 *blazoned* proclaimed (in the accompanying sonnets)   218 *affections* passions   219 *pensived* saddened; *tender* offering   222 *my . . . ender* my beginning and end, my all

223 For these of force must your oblations be,
224 Since I their altar, you enpatron me.

225 "'O, then, advance of yours that phraseless hand
     Whose white weighs down the airy scale of praise!
227 Take all these similes to your own command,
     Hallowed with sighs that burning lungs did raise.
229 What me, your minister, for you obeys,
230 Works under you; and to your audit comes
231 Their distract parcels in combinèd sums.

232 "'Lo, this device was sent me from a nun,
     Or sister sanctified, of holiest note,
234 Which late her noble suit in court did shun,
235 Whose rarest havings made the blossoms dote;
236 For she was sought by spirits of richest coat,
     But kept cold distance, and did thence remove
238 To spend her living in eternal love.

239 "'But, O my sweet, what labor is't to leave
240 The thing we have not, mast'ring what not strives,
241 Paling the place which did no form receive,
242 Playing patient sports in unconstrainèd gyves?
243 She that her fame so to herself contrives,
244 The scars of battle scapeth by the flight
245 And makes her absence valiant, not her might.

---

223 *of force* necessarily; *oblations* offerings   **224** *Since . . . enpatron me* since
you are the patron or founder of me (the altar at which they are offered)
225 *phraseless* indescribable   **227** *similes* love tokens and accompanying son-
nets   **229** *What . . . obeys* whatever pays homage to me as minister to you
230 *audit* accounting   **231** *distract* separate   **232** *device* token   **234** *suit* at-
tendance   **235** *havings* personal gifts; *blossoms* flower of the nobility   **236**
coat heraldry, descent   **238** *eternal love* love of the divine   **239** *leave* re-
nounce   **240** *mast'ring . . . strives* overcoming what does not resist   **241**
Paling . . . receive fencing an undefined area   **242** *Playing . . . gyves* pretend-
ing patiently to endure bonds that do not exist   **243** *her . . . contrives* creates
for herself the reputation for renouncing love   **244** *scars . . . flight* i.e., avoids
the wounds of a true encounter   **245** *her absence* i.e., fictitious reputation
because of absence; *might* true power (to resist love)

"'O, pardon me, in that my boast is true:
The accident which brought me to her eye
Upon the moment did her force subdue,
And now she would the cagèd cloister fly.
Religious love put out religion's eye.   250
Not to be tempted, would she be immured,
And now, to tempt all, liberty procured.   252

"'How mighty then you are, O hear me tell:
The broken bosoms that to me belong   254
Have emptied all their fountains in my well,
And mine I pour your ocean all among.
I strong o'er them, and you o'er me being strong,   257
Must for your victory us all congest,   258
As compound love to physic your cold breast.   259

"'My parts had pow'r to charm a sacred nun,   260
Who, disciplined, ay, dieted in grace,   261
Believed her eyes when they t' assail begun,   262
All vows and consecrations giving place.
O most potential love! Vow, bond, nor space   264
In thee hath neither stint, knot, nor confine,   265
For thou art all, and all things else are thine.

"'When thou impressest, what are precepts worth   267
Of stale example? When thou wilt inflame,
How coldly those impediments stand forth   269
Of wealth, of filial fear, law, kindred, fame!   270
Love's arms are peace, 'gainst rule, 'gainst sense,   271
    'gainst shame;

---

250 *Religious . . . eye* worshipful love (of the speaker) canceled her love of the
divine 252 *tempt* venture 254 *bosoms* hearts 257 *strong* victorious 258
congest gather together 259 *As . . . breast* as a medicinal compound to cure
your cold breast 261 *dieted in grace* nourished by spiritual food 262 *Be-
lieved . . . begun* put her faith in her eyes when assailed by what they saw
264 *potential* potent; *space* place (of confinement) 265 *knot* binding force
267 *impressest* conscript 269 *stand forth* appear 271 *are peace* effect
victory

And sweetens, in the suff'ring pangs it bears,
273 The aloes of all forces, shocks, and fears.

"'Now all these hearts that do on mine depend,
Feeling it break, with bleeding groans they pine;
276 And supplicant their sighs to you extend,
277 To leave the batt'ry that you make 'gainst mine,
Lending soft audience to my sweet design,
279 And credent soul to that strong-bonded oath
280 That shall prefer and undertake my troth.'

281 "This said, his wat'ry eyes he did dismount,
Whose sights till then were leveled on my face;
Each cheek a river running from a fount
With brinish current downward flowed apace.
O, how the channel to the stream gave grace!
286 Who glazed with crystal gate the glowing roses
That flame through water which their hue encloses.

"O father, what a hell of witchcraft lies
In the small orb of one particular tear!
290 But with the inundation of the eyes
What rocky heart to water will not wear!
What breast so cold that is not warmèd here,
293 O cleft effect! Cold modesty, hot wrath,
294 Both fire from hence and chill extincture hath.

"For, lo, his passion, but an art of craft,
296 Even there resolved my reason into tears;
297 There my white stole of chastity I daffed,
Shook off my sober guards and civil fears;
299 Appear to him as he to me appears,

---

273 *aloes* bitters   276 *supplicant* pleading   277 *leave the batt'ry* cease the opposition   279 *credent* believing, trusting   280 *prefer* advance; *undertake* support   281 *dismount* lower   286 *Who* which   293 *cleft* divided, double   294 *extincture* extinction   296 *resolved* dissolved   297 *daffed* doffed   299 *Appear* I appear

All melting; though our drops this diff'rence bore: 300
His poisoned me, and mine did him restore.

"In him a plenitude of subtle matter,
Applied to cautels, all strange forms receives,   303
Of burning blushes or of weeping water,
Or sounding paleness; and he takes and leaves,   305
In either's aptness, as it best deceives,   306
To blush at speeches rank, to weep at woes,
Or to turn white and sound at tragic shows;   308

"That not a heart which in his level came   309
Could scape the hail of his all-hurting aim,   310
Showing fair nature is both kind and tame;   311
And, veiled in them, did win whom he would maim.   312
Against the thing he sought he would exclaim:
When he most burned in heart-wished luxury,   314
He preached pure maid and praised cold chastity.   315

"Thus merely with the garment of a grace
The naked and concealèd fiend he covered;
That th' unexperient gave the tempter place,   318
Which, like a cherubin, above them hovered.   319
Who, young and simple, would not be so lovered?   320
Ay me! I fell, and yet do question make
What I should do again for such a sake.

"O, that infected moisture of his eye,   323
O, that false fire which in his cheek so glowed,

---

300 *drops* medicinal drops   303 *cautels* trickeries, deceits   305 *sounding* swooning; *takes and leaves* alternately employs   306 *In . . . aptness* i.e., each thing's immediate usefulness   308 *sound* swoon   309 *level* sights   310 *hail* bullets   311 *Showing . . . is* i.e., appearing to be in his nature   312 *veiled* concealed; *them* i.e., kindness and tameness   314 *luxury* lechery   315 *preached pure maid* professed virginal innocence   318 *th' unexperient . . . place* the inexperienced admitted the tempter   319 *Which . . . cherubin* who, like an angel   323 *infected* infectious

O, that forced thunder from his heart did fly,
326 O, that sad breath his spongy lungs bestowed,
327 O, all that borrowed motion seeming owed,
Would yet again betray the fore-betrayed
329 And new pervert a reconcilèd maid!"

FINIS

---

326 *spongy* diseased   327 *borrowed . . . owed* assumed behavior seemingly his own   329 *reconcilèd* penitent

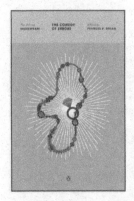